What Christian Leaders Are Saying

Changing the Stories of the World is "just what the doctor ordered" to treat the less-than-compelling Gospel story being presented by many of our churches. This book restores the Gospel to the high position it deserves in the heart of every believer and every church and is a dynamic resource for church leaders who want to equip their people to present the Gospel in its fullness.

– Clint Hall
Director of Church Relations,
The Sending Project, Olathe, Kansas

We do people a disservice when we do not tell them the Gospel in its fullness and when we present the Church as something apart from the kingdom – an afterthought or stop-gap measure until Jesus returns. *Changing the Stories of the World* is thought-provoking, enjoyable, and a much needed corrective to help the Church present a complete Gospel, to help people recognize Jesus as the King, and to submit to Him as Lord – now. It's refreshing to read something which re-evaluates the status quo in light of a hard look at Scripture. Would that more people would do so!

– Jonathan Turner
Associate Director, Key Communications

The question, "What is the Gospel?" may seem elementary. But Williams' probing answer to the question reveals that many professing Christians lack a thorough understanding of the term. His concise, well-reasoned critique of our modern conception of the Gospel, is much needed in our day. Reading this book gave me a fuller, richer, more biblical understanding of the Good News that has transformed my life and will transform the lives of those to whom God has called me to minister.

– J. Mark Horst
Teaching Pastor, Heralds of Hope, Inc.

Very nicely done! A solid and needed presentation!

– Dr. Darrell L. Bock,
Executive Director of Cultural Engagement and
Senior Research Professor of New Testament, Dallas Theological Seminary

Changing the Stories of the World

THE GOSPEL AS THE SUPERIOR STORY
IN A WORLD FULL OF FALSE STORIES

Jonathan Williams

Cover Photo: Aboriginal rock art in Northern Australia by Somners

ISBN-10: 1463588941
ISBN-13: 978-1463588946

CONTENTS

Foreword

I am privileged to be on staff with a ministry that facilitates missional awareness and networking among churches throughout the Kansas City Metro. My work has convinced me all the more of the tremendous potential that the Church has to impact society positively. However, from my vantage point, much of that potential appears to be untapped.

Having also pastored in Kansas City for many years, I have witnessed firsthand the Church gradually lose its voice in the public square, not only in my city, but across the nation. It is evident that our society, for the most part, considers the Church and its message to be outmoded and irrelevant, incapable of addressing and meeting the needs of our changing society.

I believe the disconnect between the Church and today's society can be largely attributed to the less-than-compelling story the Church is telling our society. Fifty years ago, J.B. Phillips expressed his concern when he wrote *Your God is Too Small*. Were he still alive to address the Church, I believe he would write a sequel entitled, *Your Gospel is Too Small*. However, that task has been undertaken by a pastor who offers much needed insight into the Church's lack of transformative impact in our world.

In my estimation, *Changing the Stories of the World*, is "just what the doctor ordered" to treat the less-than-compelling Gospel story being presented by many of our churches, even with the best of intentions. Written by my long-time friend and fellow pastor, Jonathan Williams, this book restores the Gospel to the high position it deserves in the heart of every believer and every church. He informs the reader early on that "changing the stories of the world is about learning that our Gospel is the Superior Story and how it changes people and nations. It is about practicing evangelism in a way that changes the stories of people and the nations in which they live."

This book is a dynamic resource for church leaders who want to equip their people to present the Gospel in its fullness. The author does an outstanding job of correctly identifying three of the most important challenges to the Gospel presented by our society. He then spends a large portion of the book showing how our Gospel, the Superior Story that God has been telling through history, overcomes each of those challenges.

It is my prayer that God will use *Changing the Stories of the World* to restore the Gospel in its fullness to our churches. It is also my prayer that this book will reignite a passion in Christ-followers to proclaim the Gospel with renewed confidence and to live out its demands through greater loving service to those around them.

Thank you, Jonathan, for this timely exhortation to the Church of our day. "To God be the glory in the Church and in Christ Jesus to all generations forever and ever. Amen!"

Clint Hall
Director of Church Relations
The Sending Project
Olathe, Kansas

Messala's Story
and Judah Ben Hur's

MY FAVORITE MOVIE IS *BEN HUR*. Have I seen it a dozen times? At least! Each viewing stirs me deeply for all its drama, passion, and adventure. In one of the opening scenes, Judah Ben-Hur and his best friend, the Roman tribune Messala, reunite after years of separation. As young boys they played and hunted together and Messala even saved Judah's life on one occasion. But the time came when Messala returned to Rome for his formal education and there he became a great soldier while Judah remained in Israel and became a prince among his people.

When they reunite, they rejoice to see each other, but something is different. It isn't just that they are no longer boys. It is that they have listened to different stories and reached for different destinies. Messala has embraced the story of Rome and its glorious empire. He is now a military tribune, a rising star in the empire, and he invites Judah Ben-Hur to come with him on his ascent to power.

But Judah refuses. He believes in the future of his people. He is following a different story, one he has followed since childhood and one for which his people would die. He takes offense that his old friend would even suggest that he betray his ancestral traditions and asks, "how can you change the ideas of an entire nation?" And to this Messala has a quick and ready reply, "You change the ideas by presenting other ideas, stronger ideas, better ideas."

Messala was right. The best way to supplant one idea is with another idea, a stronger one, a better one. The way one changes a person or nation is by presenting a narrative more powerful, more imaginative, and more satisfying than the one it is currently telling. His methods of personal, social, and political change were on the mark.

But Messala was also wrong. He had the wrong story. The world was not for Rome. It was for another Empire and another King.

I have often reflected on this scene in *Ben Hur* as I have thought about the task of world evangelism. I have come to see that God's people are called to bring about change by replacing inferior ideas, stories, and destinies with superior ones. The Gospel is our Superior Story.

Changing the Stories of the World is about learning that our Gospel is the Superior Story and how it changes people and nations. It is about practicing evangelism in a way that changes the stories of people and the nations in which they live.

But first, do we even think of the Gospel, or the Bible in this way? Do we realize that the Gospel is a Story? When I say this, I do not mean that we view it as a "nice story," a "sentimental story to make us feel good," and definitely not as a "myth" or "fairy tale with a moral" like Aesop's Fables. When I say that we approach the Bible as Story, I mean that we recognize that the Bible is the true Story of God creating the world, creating mankind, and giving him purpose. It is the story of the plan gone awry as man rebels and brings the world and its people under a curse. It is the story of God restoring mankind and the earth to its original purpose. Have you noticed this, that the Bible primarily is a narrative? Yes, it has plenty of nice sayings, important commands, decrees from God, and principles to live by, but all of these are parts of a Great Story that it tells for all who will listen. It is the Story everyone needs to hear.

Many Christians have forgotten or not learned this. Many Christians view the Bible as a book with nice sayings and important life lessons that help us solve our problems in life. The Bible will do that. But it is much more. It is the true story of our world and God invites everyone to learn that they are part of a great drama that has been unfolding on earth and to fulfill their part in it. The Story approach to the Bible is what I wish to highlight in this book.

In Chapter 1 – A World Full of Stories – I present three great challenges that face the Church today. Many of us are vaguely familiar with these challenges although we may not have heard them by the names I call them. We have employed various methods to equip God's people to combat them, but in this opening chapter I present a new way to face them – by becoming expert Storytellers who tell our Story better than the world tells its story.

In Chapter 2 – What is the Gospel? – I explain the importance of reviewing our Gospel and seeing its essence to be the Great Story. I want us to see the apostles as "good news storytellers in the ancient world." In this chapter I provide the historical background to the Gospel, and we will see that we live in a world *with competing stories*. It has always been that way. The ancient world was filled with stories of the meaning of life. In that world, one little nation was telling a very different story. It was Israel and it held to a unique storyline of how we got here, why we exist, and where we are headed. It was this story that provided the framework for the Gospel.

Chapters 3-5 are the heart of the book. In these chapters, we will look at three descriptions of the Gospel, see how they fit together, and learn how we must have this full view of the Gospel in order to combat the false stories of the world.

In Chapter 6, we look more closely at the mission of the

apostles. We will examine two texts that illustrate how the apostles connected their Gospel presentation to the Larger Story. The purpose, of course, is for us to learn from and imitate their example.

Finally, in Chapter 7, we answer the question and arrive at the true purpose of this book, as we discuss evangelism as a "story changing" activity. Our purpose is to change the stories of people. Our purpose is to change the stories of the world.

A friend recently told me something that C.S. Lewis wrote. The quote went something like this, "We should be able to explain Christianity in a way so that even if someone walks away thinking that it isn't true, they'd at least hope it was."

May this book help you become an expert Storyteller of the greatest Story in the world, the Superior Story, the True Story.

– Jonathan Williams

Chapter 1 – *A World Full of Stories*

THE WORLD IS FULL OF STORIES. Some are humorous and some are tragic. Some are full of breath-taking drama and others full of day-to-day normality.

Some stories prevail over others. They capture the imagination and the heart of the listeners. They can be fictitious and fun like a good novel, or gripping and glorious like an account of a nation's emergence from tyranny into liberty. But prevailing stories can create far more than the full-faced attention of a listener. If they are compelling, they can command the loyalty of the listeners and shape them into a force that will change the face of the earth.

Ancient empires excelled in such stories. The Greeks told a story of the culture everyone should embrace – Hellenism. The Romans told a story of the law, order, and justice they would bring to a world mired in endless conflict – the *Pax Romana*. Mystery religions of the ancient world told stories of their gods, how a normal man or woman could achieve union with those gods, and attain eternal bliss in heavenly realms.

Through the centuries, up to our own, philosophers, kings, statesmen, tyrants, and prophets have been telling stories to win the minds, hearts, and allegiance of the multitudes – sometimes for mere personal glory and sometimes to shape those multitudes into a force for change. One has to think only of Hammurabi, Homer, Virgil, Horace, Constantine, Mohammed, Charlemagne, Genghis Khan, Thomas Jefferson, Joseph Smith, Karl Marx, and Adolph Hitler.

The world is full of storytellers and stories. And people are listening.

God's people have a story. No, God's people have *The Story*, the true Story, and the Story that commends itself – like all the others – to the mind, heart, and allegiance of every person and nation on the planet. It is a story that seeks to shape those with ears to hear into a force – a force that can change hearts and alter the course of history, a force that will shine light into great darkness and replace evil with good.

We normally call this story by another name – we call it the Gospel. It is the story for which the apostles lived, suffered, and died. It is the story Jesus called Israel to believe and live for the sake of the nations. It is the story ancient prophets of Israel valiantly held to in a world of vast empires trumpeting the tales of their gods. But for many Christians, the Gospel has become far less. The Gospel has become only a personal message about how to prepare for a faraway place that we go to when life is over. Christians do not realize they hold within their hands a story of immense life-changing and world-shaping power. They hold within their grasp the Story of Power.

Many Christians are like Bilbo Baggins, the young hobbit of Middle Earth who discovers a magic ring. It saves his life and he knows he has something special. But that is all he knows. He lives his life happily in the Shire, using his Ring from time to time to play tricks on people or to disappear when he sees an annoying acquaintance on the road ahead of him. The Ring is only for his personal convenience and safety. Meanwhile, world-shaping events are unfolding in Middle Earth to which he is oblivious. And he is also oblivious to something else – the world-shaping events all have to do with The Ring that he keeps tucked away in his pocket or hidden in a drawer.

The Gospel is unlike the Ring in that it is a force for good. But like the Ring, it is the most potent, world-shaping force imaginable. The Gospel is the power of God to change people, families, communities, and nations. As Paul said, the Gospel is the power of God for salvation. But too many Christians keep it tucked away safely in their vest and pull it out only for personal comfort or emergencies. In the meantime, world shaping events unfold around us as Dark Riders – enemies of the Gospel – spread their influence around the globe.

Dark Riders

What are these Dark Riders, these challenges that assail Christianity in our day? I will identify three. The first enemy that assails us is what I call "Generic Theism." On the day that I first wrote these words, the president of the United States did something of earth shaking significance – he lit a candle for a Hindu god in the White House. The press hardly noticed. It was mostly a non-story. After all, he was not converting to Hinduism or even trying to influence the nation toward it. Yet this non-story, an act of toleration toward immigrants with a completely different worldview and philosophy about reality was, instead, an unwitting act of great treachery with implications far more insidious than most people realized. He was affirming Generic Theism – *you believe in "a god", I believe in "a god", others believe in some type of higher power. It doesn't matter what your belief is as long as you have faith and seek to benefit others.* This is Generic Theism.

A second challenge that assails the church is an internal enemy. I call it "Fortune Cookie Christianity." You know about fortune cookies. You are at a Chinese restaurant. You have enjoyed a good meal with friends, but there is a ritual to perform at the end of the meal. Your server brings you a small tray with the bill and a fortune cookie for all. Everyone eagerly tears off the wrapper, breaks the cookie, reads their fortune, and shares it with others – a fitting and fun end to a great meal.

Unfortunately, that's the way many Christians approach The Book that contains The Narrative of Power. The Bible is a book of "sayings," "promises," "principles," and "commands" – *only*. Kind of like fortune cookie sayings. We read them, memorize them, pray about them, claim them, and sometimes obey them – all good. But too often we don't realize these individual sayings are pieces of a larger narrative that exists to change people … and the world. Far too many Christians treat the Bible as a book of "Fortune Cookie" sayings. Their faith never rises above the "sayings" and never connects to the Story of Power, and they go on their merry way in their Fortune Cookie Christianity.

A third challenge I call "The Mystic Messiah." If Generic Theism is true and all gods are roughly equal, if the Bible is merely a handbook of nice sayings with no connection to a narrative, then Jesus of Nazareth loses his uniqueness. He loses his pivotal place in the Story of Power and our tendency will be to view him through the lens of the spirit of the age – as a mystic who spoke about eternal realities to help people find their true self, connect with the oneness of everything, and one day escape this corrupt planet and merge with the Divine in heavenly realms forever.

I have written *Changing the Stories of the World* to alert God's people to the challenges in front of us and to equip them to engage these challenges. In the pages of this book, you will discover that one of the primary characteristics of the Gospel is that it connects to a larger story God's spokesmen have been telling for centuries. It is the story of *The Gospel of the Kingdom of God*. The Kingdom of God is the controlling narrative of Scripture[1] and God desires his people to rediscover this Narrative of Power in order to rise above Fortune Cookie Christianity.

I intend for my book also to be an antidote to the weakness of Generic Theism, and I will do it by highlighting another characteristic of the Gospel message which biblical writers frequently call *The Gospel of God*. They call it this because their mission was to rescue the world from Generic Theism and bring it into Specific Theism, or, what theologians call Covenantal Monotheism – the abandonment of all false gods

---

[1] In 1994, I introduced my Master's Thesis, "The Kingdom of God: Present or Postponed" by pointing to the centrality of the kingdom of God in Scripture. The work of Kenneth C. Barker was helpful as he quoted no less than 17 authors who pointed to the kingdom as the centerpiece of theology. See pp. 314-318, "The Scope and Center of Old and New Testament Theology and Hope" in *Dispensationalism, Israel, and the Church.* Barker said: "It seems clear, then, that although there are several great theological themes in the Bible, the central focus of biblical theology is the rule of God, the kingdom of God or the interlocking concepts of kingdom and covenant (but not covenant alone). At the very least, God's rule is a dominant theological theme in the Bible" p. 318.

A recent statement on the centrality of the kingdom is in the work by Paul G. Hiebert, *Anthropological Insights for Missionaries.* On page 18 he states, "The center of Christ's message was the kingdom of God, wherein God is still at work in creation and in history to redeem the world unto himself…. The scope of God's mission is not only the kingdom in heaven, but also his kingdom on earth. Although it has to do with the eternal destiny of humans, it also deals with their well-being on earth – with peace, justice, liberty, health, provision, and righteousness."

and the worship of the true God who is eternal, who created the heavens and the earth, and who entered into a relationship of love with one nation for the sake of the world.

Finally, I intend this book to engage a third challenge which I call The Mystic Messiah. We do this by affirming *The Gospel of the Lord Jesus Christ*. Each of those words, Lord – Jesus – Christ is filled with deep significance. We will explain why as the book unfolds and show how it counteracts The Mystic Messiah idea. When we rediscover and affirm all the dimensions of the Gospel, Jesus Christ can then take his rightful, glorious place as the unique covenant keeping, curse bearing, death defeating, Spirit empowering, enthroned-at-the-right-hand-of-God Lord of all. Quite a difference between this and being a writer of fortune cookie sayings. There is no one like him. There is no story like his story and the Story of Power that we call the Gospel.

Change the Stories of the World

As I listen to news reports with history shaping and culture changing implications in faraway places and in our own country, I feel the Holy Spirit pressing something repeatedly into my heart – "you must change the stories of the world." Guns will not change the stories of the world. They can force bad people to stop doing bad things but that's as far as they go. They create an outward peace but they do not change people's deeply entrenched heart beliefs.

Elections will not change the narratives of the world. They impose the will of the majority upon the minority (better than using a gun), but people in the minority rarely change their viewpoints. Instead, they redouble their efforts to become the majority and impose their political will. Few people in the meantime stop to examine what they believe and why they believe as they do. Few change their viewpoints, their stories.

What will change the stories of people and the world? Only a Story more powerful, more compelling, more imaginative, and more demanding than all others can replace the false stories that run rampant through the place where God made man to live. But we cannot change the world's stories unless we know our Story, and when we know it with all its life changing, world changing, history changing power, we will then find ourselves equipped to take our God-intended role in life and history.

We must become expert storytellers like Jesus and the apostles and we must become totally committed storytellers -- because our lives are part of the Great Story. Only total commitment to learning, living, and telling the Story will make a difference in the world. The Gospel is the true Story of Power that will change people and one day change the planet. God is asking us to rediscover the Gospel in all its dimensions for his glory and for the advance of his reign on the earth. But in order to change the narratives of the world from its false stories to the true, we must first pause and examine our message. We must ask, "What is the Gospel?"

Chapter 2 – *What is the Gospel?*

IS IT REALLY WORTH OUR WHILE TO ASK THE QUESTION, "What is the Gospel?" Am I being demeaning to some and perhaps creating suspicion in others; "What do you mean, 'What is the Gospel?' I've been sharing it for years. Are you calling my work into question? Are you asking so you can sneak in something extra and distort it in some way?"

Christian history is full of such attempts, and some of us know what it is to deal with cults or fringe elements that twist the Gospel to advance personal agendas or heretical ideas. But asking this question is a biblical practice. Paul, after his first missionary journey, re-examined the Gospel he was preaching.

> [1]Then after an interval of fourteen years I went up again to Jerusalem with Barnabas, taking Titus along also. [2]It was because of a revelation that I went up; and I submitted to them the Gospel which I preach among the Gentiles, but I did so in private to those who were of reputation, for fear that I might be running, or had run, in vain.[2]

---

[2] Galatians 2:1-2

If Paul exhibited such humility and carefulness, how much more should we. But once Paul knew he had his story right, he then became vigilant to guard the Gospel. Galatians 2 instructs us again. This time Paul tells a story of compromise *among the apostles*!

> ¹¹But when Cephas came to Antioch, I opposed him to his face, because he stood condemned. ¹²For prior to the coming of certain men from James, he used to eat with the Gentiles; but when they came, he began to withdraw and hold himself aloof, fearing the party of the circumcision. ¹³The rest of the Jews joined him in hypocrisy, with the result that even Barnabas was carried away by their hypocrisy. ¹⁴But when I saw that **they were not straightforward about the truth of the Gospel**, I said to Cephas in the presence of all ….

None other than Peter and Barnabas were compromising the Gospel – at least in practice. They were yielding to the pressure of Jewish Christians who believed it was wrong for Jews to share a meal with Gentiles, even if those Gentiles were believers in Jesus. We should take Peter's and Barnabas' failure as a warning to reflect upon the Gospel we preach and practice. As we examine Paul's letter to the Galatians more closely, we discover even more warnings. Galatians is his letter to a region of churches to warn against a different Gospel (1:6), a distortion of the Gospel (1:7), and a Gospel contrary to apostolic authority (1:8-9).

About this time, the apostles convened the first church council to clarify the Gospel message[3] and subsequent letters by all the apostles warned against false doctrine, false Gospels, false apostles, and behavior inconsistent with the Gospel.[4] Obviously, it is worth our while to ask and answer

---

[3] See Peter's turning point remarks in Acts 15:6-11.
[4] Romans 16:17-18; Colossians 2:8; 1 Corinthians 12:3; 2 Corinthians 11:3-4; 1 Timothy 1:3-4; 4:1; 6:3-4; 2 Timothy 2:15-18; Titus 1:13-14; 2 Peter 2; 1 John 2:18-27; 4:1-6; Jude 1; Revelation 2:14-15; 2:20-24

the question, "What is the Gospel?"

Make no mistake, I believe the Gospel evangelicals preach is in line with apostolic authority, but I do have a major concern. I believe many have forgotten, unwittingly neglected, or never learned some crucial characteristics of the Gospel with an unwanted result. While we preach the true Gospel, we preach it in a truncated form that hinders the Gospel message from working out its full implications in the lives of people and the nations in which they live. It leaves people and nations spiritually anemic and cut off from God's full strength. Like a fresh transfusion of blood, a re-examination of the Gospel can refocus and re-energize our ministry. And why shouldn't this happen? The Gospel is, after all, the most powerful message in the world. Consider these facts about the amazing nature of the message God has given us.

- The Gospel we preach is the same message the prophets pointed to,[5] Jesus inaugurated,[6] and the apostles took worldwide.[7] This should motivate us. We are standing in the same tradition with the same

---

[5] Peter said the prophets spoke about the grace we experience – 1 Peter 1:10-12. Peter, in his second recorded sermon in Acts, said all the prophets from Samuel forward spoke about the days that Peter and his fellow apostles were experiencing – Acts 3:24. Paul said the Scriptures were proclaiming the Gospel to Abraham when God promised that He would bless all the nations through him – Galatians 3:8 with Genesis 12:3. John the Baptist, the last and greatest of the Old Testament prophets preached the Gospel – Luke 3:18.

[6] Luke 20:1 – "On one of the days while He was teaching the people in the temple and preaching the Gospel, the chief priests and the scribes with the elders confronted Him." See also Matthew 11:5; Luke 4:18; 7:22; and 9:6.

[7] Acts 8:25 – "So when they had solemnly testified and spoken the word of the Lord, they started back to Jerusalem, and were preaching the Gospel to many villages of the Samaritans." See also 8:40; 14:7, 15, 21; 15:7; 16:10.

purpose as holy men, prophets, apostles, and our Savior. God has not given us a different message or an inferior message. It is not as if his Son and apostles had top security clearance to see secret messages that we cannot see. We have the same message and mission they had.

- This message is so important everyone on the planet must hear it – every nation, tribe, tongue, and people.[8]
- This message is so important, Paul, our supreme apostolic example,[9] said that he did all things for the sake of the Gospel,[10] and it was the cause he lived for.[11] In other words, our Gospel is worth everything – including our lives.

The Gospel is the most glorious message in the world. No drama ever written by great novelists surpasses it. No imagination of fantasy or science fiction writers can match it. The adventures of heroic men and women succeeding against insurmountable odds pale in comparison to the achievements of Jesus Christ. The discoveries of explorers and archaeologists, even the greatest who have opened the tombs of buried kings and uncovered lost and mysterious civilizations are trivial compared to the doors Jesus Christ has opened. Paul described his message as "the glorious Gospel of the blessed God,"[12] and said that Christ "abolished death and brought life and immortality to light through the Gospel."[13]

Did you catch those amazing phrases? In 1 Timothy 1:11

---

[8] Revelation 14:6

[9] 1 Corinthians 4:16; 11:1; Philippians 3:17

[10] 1 Corinthians 9:23

[11] Philippians 4:3

[12] 1 Timothy 1:11

[13] 2 Timothy 1:9-10

Paul describes his Gospel as *the glorious Gospel*. In 2 Timothy 1:10 he says Jesus Christ has *opened the door to immortality*. Some people get excited when an explorer opens the tomb of a famous king – the place of a dead man. Jesus opened the door to immortality! Could any message be more important or exciting? This is why we must study, review, and clarify our understanding of the Gospel.

I hope to take a familiar subject and refresh every reader with it. I also hope to expand everyone's understanding of the Gospel in order to see it in all its dimensions. In subsequent chapters, we will do the following:

1. Examine the New Testament usage of Gospel. We will discover the Gospel in all its dimensions and learn how the full measure of the Gospel equips us to engage the challenges we face today.
2. Look at the apostles as storytellers. In this I am not referring to a speaking style but to their conscious effort to link their message with the Larger Story of the God of creation and the God of Israel.
3. Describe and define the Gospel.
4. Take initial steps in learning how to change the stories of people and nations.

For now, it is important to look at root meanings of the word, Gospel, and see how the ancient secular and the Hebrew world used these words. We will discover that *Gospel* was a common word describing good news passing from one community to another as the "Gospel messengers" told their stories.

Good News Stories and Storytellers

The primary word for Gospel is *euanggelion* (good news, Gospel). We translate two verbs, *euanggelizo* and *euanggelizomai* as "to bring or announce good news, proclaim, and preach." The noun *euanggelistes* refers to "the proclaimer of glad tidings" or "an evangelist."

Etymologists find these words as early as the writings of Homer and point out that they derive from the more basic word *angelos* (messenger) and *angello* (to announce). They referred to one who brought "a message of victory or other political or personal news that causes joy."[14] In other words, they were telling a story! They were telling a story of events that had transpired in a distant place that had joyful consequences for their cities and lives.

Writers in the Hellenistic period used these words for someone who announced prophetic oracles or for the appearance of a "divine man" who would bring joy to a city or community. Oracles contained promises (*epangelia* – from the same word family as Gospel). The promises could be promises of divine visitations, of a coming golden age, or of good fortune that would come one's way. The stories or visitations could bring joy or warning to a community.

We see this played out in Luke's account of Paul healing the lame man in Lystra and the crowds honoring Paul as Hermes and Barnabas as Zeus: "The gods have become like men and have come down to us."[15] The people saw Paul and Barnabas as messengers coming to their city with good news. Indeed they were, but a very different kind of messenger with a very different kind of good news.

Such promises also took on political dimensions. This is not surprising in light of the ancient world's union of religion and state. Our modern notion of the "separation of church and state" would have been incomprehensible to them.

---

[14] Ulrich Becker, Dictionary of New Testament Theology, Volume 2, Colin Brown, ed., "Gospel", p. 107.
[15] Acts 14:11-13

"News of the divine ruler's birth, coming of age, or enthronement, and also his speeches, decrees and acts are *glad tidings* which bring the much hoped-for fulfillment of the world's longing for happiness and peace."[16]

A great example of this is a speech in the year 9 BC by the Roman proconsul Paulus Fabius Maximus. He introduced the imperial cult to the province of Asia by marking September 23, the birth day of Augustus, as the new beginning for their civil year. Listen to his description of Augustus' birth. Notice how he presents it as good news for the community, the new narrative everyone is to believe. Notice also the religious overtones which I have put in bold.

> It is a day which we may justly count as equivalent to **the beginning of everything** – if not in itself and in its own nature, at any rate in the benefits it brings – inasmuch as it has **restored the shape of everything** that was failing and turning into misfortune, and has **given a new look to the Universe** at a time when it would gladly have welcomed destruction if Caesar had not been born to be **the common blessing of all men....**

> Whereas the Providence (*pronoia*) which has ordered the whole of our life, showing concern and zeal, has ordained **the most perfect consummation** for human life by giving to it Augustus, by filling him with virtue for doing the work of a benefactor among men, and by sending in him, as it were, **a savior for us** and those who come after us, to make war to cease, to create order everywhere ... and whereas the birthday of **the God** [Augustus] was the beginning for the world of the **glad tidings** [in the Greek, the 'Evangel'] that have come to men through him ...

> Paulus Fabius Maximus, the proconsul of the province ... has devised a way of honouring Augustus hitherto unknown to the Greeks, which is, that **the reckoning of time for the course**

---

[16] Becker, 108

of human life would begin with his birth.[17]

"Listen to my story," Maximus was saying. "A savior has been born! Let us create a new calendar! Let us date everything from the birth of Augustus! This ruler of the world has brought us peace. The climax of all history has arrived. The one especially filled by God is on the earth and we owe him our allegiance and worship!"

Most people know Rome was ruling the world at that time. What they do not know is that Rome was also telling a story to inspire (and demand when inspiration did not work) the allegiance of all men. N.T. Wright notes,

> It was not by military force alone that Augustus consolidated his power, or that his successors maintained it. It has been shown in great detail that from the beginning the empire used every available means in art, architecture, literature and culture in general – everything from tiny coins to the rebuilding of entire city centres – to communicate to the Roman people near and far the message that Augustus's rise to power was the great new moment for which Rome, and indeed the whole world, had been waiting.[18]

No wonder Messala tried to convince Ben Hur to join him. Messala had drunk deeply from the well of Rome's wonders and its purpose to bring order, prosperity, and blessing to the world. He had bought into the Gospel of Rome, that its empire and emperor would fill every need and bring peace and prosperity to all. This was the good news, the Gospel of Rome, the message Messala was preaching to his childhood friend, Ben Hur, "join me in this glorious mission that will bring peace to the world and blessing for all. Hail Caesar."

And Ben Hur said "No." Why did he refuse Messala's offer? It was because he believed another story – the story of the

---

[17] Becker, p. 108
[18] N.T. Wright, *Paul and the Faithfulness of God*, p. 294.

world's true Lord. He believed the story the prophets had been telling his people for centuries. He believed in an Anointed One who would come – and his name was not Caesar. As we read the novel or watch the epic tale, we see choices made by both men with long-lasting and sometimes devastating consequences because the world can have only one Lord and one prevailing story. People must choose carefully.

This world of empires in conflict and competing claims for allegiance and loyalty was the world of ancient prophets and apostles. We must not think of them as men who lived in isolation from the great events happening around them, as if they were armchair theologians with leisure time for reflection of great ideas. It was a world like the one the prophet Daniel described – a world where men boasted great things, a world where men blasphemously reached for divinity and used every military, political, and religious means to advance their monstrous agendas. N.T. Wright again describes the reality in which the early church preached its Gospel.

> By the end of the century, in the middle of which Paul came through the eastern empire preaching the message of Jesus, these developments had produced a new civic and religious reality. The highest honour a city could now hope for was to become *neokoros*, temple-guardian for the *Sebastoi*, the Augustus family. Worshipping the emperors was well on the way to becoming a central and vital aspect not only of life in general but of civic and municipal identity.[19]

> [The] … imperial cult … gave shape and body to ordinary life, especially urban life with its feasts and banquets, its public games and festivals. Indeed, it can be argued that imperial cult was a significant factor in the development of the cities themselves in the period, creating and sustaining new patterns

---

[19] Wright, 341

of civic life in regions not previously urbanized.[20]

This was the controlling narrative of the ancient world – a Gospel of world empires which permeated every facet of life. This is the world where the apostles proclaimed a different narrative, a different Gospel, a different Lord – *the Gospel of Jesus Christ*. One can easily see the risks they, and countless others, took in proclaiming another king besides Caesar![21] Many paid the ultimate price for their faithfulness.[22] They were, in effect, dethroning an abomination and putting the rightful king on the throne of the world. If they had been content to add their story into the mix of the Caesar story and the lesser mystery religion stories of the day, the authorities would have left them alone. But they knew that the narrative of God's Kingdom and of Jesus Christ was incompatible with and subversive to the story the Roman Empire was telling. Their Gospel inherently called it into question. This is a far cry from seeing the apostles as bringing a message of love and brotherhood for all or preaching a message of how people can go to heaven when they die. Of course, it includes those elements, but we shall see that the Gospel is far, far bigger than those messages.

The Light of the World

In the midst of these ancient world stories about gods, humans becoming gods, and loyalty to empires, one nation stood apart from the others. For centuries, it had dared to tell another story while one empire replaced another on the world stage. Of course, I am talking about Israel – the people with whom God entered into a covenant relationship. A few

---

[20] Wright, 341-342

[21] Acts 17:6-7

[22] "And they overcame him because of the blood of the Lamb and because of the word of their testimony, and they did not love their life even when faced with death," Revelation 12:11.

words, then, about the Old Testament background for the Gospel.

The Septuagint, the Greek translation of the Hebrew Bible uses the Greek words noted above to translate a family of Hebrew words that mean *reward for a messenger, glad tidings, to announce, tell, and publish.*[23] The Old Testament writers used them generically to speak of passing news from one locale to another, but theologically they used them to proclaim "Yahweh's universal victory over the world and his kingly rule."[24] The kingdoms of the world with their rebellion and blasphemy would not prevail. God's kingdom would win out and he would restore his authority on the earth. This is the heart of David's cry in Psalm 9:19-20: "Arise O Lord, do not let man prevail. Let the nations be judged before You. Put them in fear, O Lord. Let the nations know that they are but men."

God entrusted Israel with this good news for the world – their God, the God of Abraham, Isaac, and Jacob was the true God. He was not a tribal deity limited to one people and one land like the gods of the nations surrounding them. Nor was he the highest god in the pantheon of gods, like Zeus. He was the only God. All the others were frauds. The Jews celebrated their God and their special role to tell the nations about him in many places. Psalm 96 is a good example.

---

[23] Becker, p. 108
[24] Becker, p. 109

¹Sing to the LORD a new song; Sing to the LORD, all the earth. ²Sing to the LORD, bless His name. Proclaim good tidings of His salvation from day to day. ³Tell of His glory among the nations, His wonderful deeds among all the peoples. ⁴For great is the LORD and greatly to be praised; He is to be feared above all gods. ⁵For all the gods of the peoples are idols, but the LORD made the Heavens. ⁶Splendor and majesty are before Him, strength and beauty are in His sanctuary. ⁷Ascribe to the LORD, O families of the peoples, ascribe to the LORD glory and strength.

⁸Ascribe to the LORD the glory of His name; Bring an offering and come into His courts. ⁹Worship the LORD in holy attire. Tremble before Him, all the earth. ¹⁰Say among the nations, "The LORD reigns; Indeed, the world is firmly established, it will not be moved; He will judge the peoples with equity." ¹¹Let the heavens be glad, and let the earth rejoice; Let the sea roar, and all it contains. ¹²Let the field exult, and all that is in it. Then all the trees of the forest will sing for joy ¹³Before the LORD, for He is coming, for He is coming to judge the earth. He will judge the world in righteousness and the peoples in His faithfulness.

Let's make some observations on this psalm.

- The writer exhorts *the whole earth* to sing to the Lord and bless his name (v. 1). It is a message for the whole world to hear.
- The whole earth should proclaim glad tidings (Gospel) of his salvation every day (v. 2).
- All the gods of the world are frauds but the God of Israel made all things (4-5). This would be highly controversial in the ancient world and would call empires into question for their state was based upon their religion.

- No one exists like Israel's God (6) and all peoples are to worship him only (7-9).
- God's people are to proclaim among the nations that Yahweh, the Lord, reigns (10). The other gods are imposters whether they are idols of wood, stone, or human flesh strutting across the earth. The God of Israel was God alone.
- He, the Creator, would come to reclaim the earth, judge the nations, and reign over all. His return would bring liberation to the planet and everything in creation will sing and exult before him (10-13).

This was the good news Isaiah proclaimed to the Jewish exiles in Babylon. The gods of Babylon appeared stronger than Yahweh, but they would fall because they were "nothings." The Babylonians may have destroyed Jerusalem and taken the people of God into slavery, but they would be released, be restored to the land, and re-enter their purpose of proclaiming truth to the world. Here is how Isaiah put it:

> How lovely on the mountains are the feet of him who brings good news, who announces peace and brings good news of happiness, who announces salvation, and says to Zion, "Your God reigns!"[25]

The God of Israel reigns, not the gods of the nations of the world. This was the light Israel was to shine in the darkness of the world that had exchanged the true God for objects made of wood and stone. This was the light Israel was to shine in a world that created civilizations built upon man-made religions where men claimed that they were the bearers of order, peace, and justice for all. In such an environment, it is easy to see why the apostolic proclamation often met with resistance and persecution. The Gospel called these civilizations and empires into question.

---

[25] Isaiah 52:7

You may have noticed that I did not answer the question posed in the title, "What is the Gospel?" We have some more groundwork to complete. We have examined the background of the word, Gospel, and the way it was used in the ancient world. Now we must examine the various ways the apostles used the word.

Chapter 3 – *The Gospel of God*

O NE OF THE FEATURES OF THE NEW TESTAMENT VERSES that use the word Gospel is the several descriptors that go with it. By far, most verses speak only of *the Gospel*, but many others add a word or phrase providing clues to answer our question – *What is the Gospel*. I have discovered eight basic descriptors.

1. **The Gospel of God**[26] – Paul, a bond-servant of Christ Jesus, called as an apostle, set apart for the Gospel of God – Romans 1:1

2. **The Gospel of the Kingdom**[27] – Jesus was going throughout all Galilee, teaching in their synagogues and proclaiming the Gospel of the kingdom, and healing every kind of disease and every kind of sickness among the people. – Matthew 4:23

---

[26] See also Mark 1:14; Romans 15:16; 2 Corinthians 11:7; 1 Thessalonians 2:2, 8-9; 1 Peter 4:17. See also 1 Timothy 1:11 – *the Gospel of the blessed God* and Revelation 14:6 – *an eternal Gospel.*

[27] See also Matthew 4:23; 9:35; 24:14 (compare with Mark 13:10 – Gospel only); Luke 16:16; and Acts 8:12. See Chapter 4 for more details on the Gospel of the kingdom.

3. **The Gospel of your salvation** – In Him, you also, after listening to the message of truth, the Gospel of your salvation – having also believed, you were sealed in Him with the Holy Spirit of promise. – Ephesians 1:13

4. **The Gospel of peace** – and having shod your feet with the preparation of the Gospel of peace. – Ephesians 6:15

5. **The Gospel according to the power of God** – Therefore do not be ashamed of the testimony of our Lord or of me His prisoner, but join with me in suffering for the Gospel according to the power of God. – 2 Timothy 1:8

6. **The Gospel of Jesus Christ/of His Son/of Christ/of our Lord Jesus**[28] – The beginning of the Gospel of Jesus Christ, the Son of God. – Mark 1:1

7. **The Gospel of the grace of God** – But I do not consider my life of any account as dear to myself, so that I may finish my course and the ministry which I received from the Lord Jesus, to testify solemnly of the Gospel of the grace of God. – Acts 20:24

8. **The Gospel of the promise made to the fathers** – And we preach to you the good news of the promise made to the fathers. – Acts 13:32

---

[28] **Of Jesus Christ** – Mark 1:1
Of His Son – Romans 1:9; (see also 1:1-4)
Of Christ – Romans 15:19; 16:25; 1 Corinthians 9:12; 2 Corinthians 2:12; 4:4; 9:13; 10:14; Galatians 1:7; Philippians 1:17; 1 Thessalonians 3:2
Of our Lord Jesus – 2 Thessalonians 1:8

The descriptors supply shades of meaning to the one Gospel. These different shades are often lost or minimalized in our modern presentation of the Gospel. It is important that we recover them. For example, the Gospel brings peace between God and man and between man and man; therefore, we call it *the Gospel of peace*. But when Paul, quoting Isaiah, speaks of the Gospel in this way, he has a more comprehensive meaning in mind than we normally do. In the ancient world, the promise of peace was not just for internal happiness. It was a socio-political hope. Remember what Fabius Maximus said about Augustus? He was the divinely appointed agent for whom the entire world waited who would end the destruction that came with war and bring order and blessing to the world – in other words, *peace*. We must also remember the context in which Isaiah, the prophet whom Paul quoted, spoke. He was announcing deliverance from Babylon when he said:

> How lovely on the mountains are the feet of him who brings good news, who announces peace and brings good news of happiness, who announces salvation and says to Zion, "Your God reigns!"

The good news of peace preached by prophets and apostles was a rival story to the ones told by ancient empires. It was not just a message of internal peace, although that is important as well. We should note the same emphasis when we read the phrase, *the Gospel of your salvation*. We hear the word, "salvation," and think immediately of being saved from the judgment because of our sins. And rightly so for the *Gospel of salvation* brings deliverance from the judgment against our sin. But salvation was never individual salvation only. The Hebrew concept included the restoration of all things.[29]

But this is getting ahead of ourselves. Our purpose at this point is to discover the different shades of meaning for the one Gospel, discover how they fit together, and place them together into a comprehensible story that we are to tell the world. We will also learn that when we fit them together into a coherent narrative, they will equip us in a new and powerful way to engage the enemies that face the Church today and empower us to share the Gospel with greater authority.

In this and the following two chapters, I will seek to answer these questions by focusing on three primary descriptors of the Gospel, the Gospel of God, the Gospel of the Kingdom of God, and the Gospel of our Lord Jesus Christ. We are so accustomed to speaking of the Gospel of the Lord Jesus Christ that we have neglected or not carefully observed these other dimensions of the Gospel. I am not speaking of "other Gospels." Paul pronounces anathema upon men or angels who present a different message.[30] But I am speaking of verses where the apostles speak of the Gospel in a broader, fuller way. We might say that the Gospel of Christ is the heart of the Gospel message but these other dimensions of the Gospel provide the flesh and bones in which the heart resides.

Paul's Mission

Paul introduces his greatest letter, the letter to the church at Rome, with these words.

Paul, a bond-servant of Christ Jesus, called as an apostle, set

---

[29] See for example, Isaiah 25:8-9; 33:1-6; 51:5-6; Jeremiah 3:23; Habakkuk 3:13; Zechariah 9:9-10.

[30] Galatians 1:7-10

apart for the Gospel of God, which He promised beforehand through His prophets in the holy Scriptures.[31]

Paul begins with a description of himself and his mission – he is a bondservant of Christ Jesus, gifted to be an apostle, and set apart for *the Gospel of God*. He does not say the Gospel of Christ, but the Gospel of God. We could dismiss this as an unusual choice of words with little significance except that he repeats this emphasis at a key moment[32] in his epistle.

> But I have written very boldly to you on some points so as to remind you again, because of the grace that was given me from God, to be a minister of Christ Jesus to the Gentiles, ministering as a priest the Gospel of God, so that my offering of the Gentiles may become acceptable, sanctified by the Holy Spirit.[33]

Paul speaks of God gracing him with the gift of apostleship so that he could proclaim Christ Jesus to the Gentiles. Then, he uses the picture of an Old Testament priest offering a sacrifice in the Temple. Instead of an animal, Paul offers Gentiles to God as an act of worship, and he describes his priesthood in this way – *ministering as a priest the Gospel of God*.

Notice what Paul wrote to the Gentiles in Thessalonica who believed his message. "For they themselves report about us what kind of a reception we had with you, and how you turned to God from idols to serve a living and true God."[34] Just a few sentences later, Paul described his message as *the Gospel of God* in 2:2 and 2:8-9.

---

[31] Romans 1:1

[32] It is a key moment because Paul has just climaxed the epistle with his call for Jew and Gentile to accept one another in the Body (15:7) and by providing the biblical basis for his mission to the Gentiles.

[33] Romans 15:15-16

[34] 1 Thessalonians 1:9

²but after we had already suffered and been mistreated in Philippi, as you know, we had the boldness in our God to speak to you the Gospel of God amid much opposition.

⁸Having so fond an affection for you, we were well-pleased to impart to you not only the Gospel of God but also our own lives, because you had become very dear to us. ⁹For you recall, brethren, our labor and hardship, how working night and day so as not to be a burden to any of you, we proclaimed to you the Gospel of God.

What is the Gospel of God? Is it just an uncareful exchange of words on Paul's part where he does not have any specific point to make – sometimes he uses the word *Christ* and sometimes *God*? Or, did he have a purpose and different shade of meaning to present? I believe it is the latter and that it provided a framework for the Gospel of Christ. The Gospel of God is the good news that God really does exist. He is one. He is all powerful. He is the creator. He reveals himself to his creation and has a plan for the earth and every person on it. This God is holy, and he is full of love. As a Jew, this was central to Paul's identity. Twice a day devout Jews would recite the Shema. "Hear O Israel, the LORD is our God. The LORD is one." But this was much more than a "religious confession." N.T. Wright notes:

> …the most intimate and personal way of taking on oneself 'the yoke of the kingdom of heaven' was the praying of the *Shema*, two or more times a day. Invoking YHWH as the 'one God' and determining to love him with mind, heart and *nephesh*, life itself, meant a total commitment to the sovereignty of this one God, the creator, the God of Israel, and a repudiation of all the idols of paganism and the cruel empires which served them.³⁵

> From the beginning, Jewish monotheism was a way of saying 'no' to this claim (of sovereignty by idols and empires),

---

³⁵ Wright, p. 630

whether from Egypt, Babylon, Greece, Syria, Rome or anywhere else, and a way of claiming instead … that the God who made all the earth would set up his own kingdom, would draw his own line through the world, refocusing the edge-lured minds of his human creatures, in his own way and time.[36]

Paul's twice-a-day confession of Israel's God as the solitary, unique God in a world full of gods and goddesses was reinforced by his conversion because he believed that the one true God had acted supremely and decisively in Jesus of Nazareth to re-stake his claim in this world and to inaugurate his reign and the new creation for which all mankind longed.

The Gospel is first, good news about who God is and what he is like. This would be an important message in the ancient world (as well as our own) where atheism was the exception and belief in "God", or more accurately, the gods, was the norm. Paul, therefore, preached that the whole world must turn from their idols and embrace the God of Israel, the true God. This is what he preached at Lystra (Acts 14:8-18), at Athens (Acts 17:22-31) and presumably every other city to any Gentile who would listen. Paul, therefore, was continuing the mission of Israel to testify to the world that its God was the true God, which is why he referred to himself as a Jewish priest in the temple offering the formerly idolatrous and now repentant Gentiles as an act of worship to the true God.

Jesus' Mission

Mark, at the beginning of his Gospel, introduced Jesus' ministry with these words,

---

[36] Wright, p. 631

"Now after John had been taken into custody, Jesus came into Galilee, preaching the Gospel of God."[37]

Why would Jesus, coming to his covenant people who already knew the one true God preach this message? It is because Jesus was affirming to his people that their God, the true God, was about to act in fulfillment of the promises he made to them. We must remember that though many Jews had come back to the land, their exile was not really over.[38] The Babylonians were replaced with the Persians and the Persians with the Greeks. Empires changed and Israel remained under their dominion for hundreds of years. In 163 BC the Jews, after a time of terrible suffering defeated Antiochus IV and re-gained sovereignty, yet it was only for a brief period of 100 years. When the Roman general Pompey marched into Jerusalem in 63 BC, they found themselves once again under the heels of a pagan empire, this time, Rome.

It appeared that the gods of the Gentiles were stronger than the God of Israel. If the gods were not seducing the people with their ancient sexual fertility rites, they were enslaving the people through the advance of their empires. But the people held firmly to their conviction that their God would act and reverse this condition in the world. To this, the promises of the prophets pointed. When Daniel told Nebuchadnezzar about his dream and the statue of gold, silver, bronze, and iron and clay he told him that these represented the kingdoms of the world and that these kingdoms would be destroyed.

---

[37] Mark 1:14

[38] Note the prayer of the priests in Nehemiah 9:36-37, "Behold, we are slaves today, and as to the land which You gave to our fathers to eat of its fruit and its bounty, behold, we are slaves in it. Its abundant produce is for the kings whom you have set over us because of our sins. They also rule over our bodies and over our cattle as they please, so we are in great distress."

In the days of those kings the God of heaven will set up a kingdom which will never be destroyed, and that kingdom will not be left for another people. It will crush and put an end to all these kingdoms, but it will itself endure forever. Inasmuch as you saw that a stone was cut out of the mountain without hands and that it crushed the iron, the bronze, the clay, the silver and the gold, the great God has made known to the kingdom what will take place in the future. So the dream is true and its interpretation is trustworthy.[39]

Have we ever considered the courage it took for Daniel to say these words to the tyrant, Nebuchadnezzar? Daniel's words were not just an interpretation of an obscure dream. They were promises, guarantees that God's kingdom would overthrow the kingdoms of the world, including Nebuchadnezzar's. This is a far cry from the way we sometimes think of biblical promises. Daniel wasn't talking about a religious experience or the hope of heaven. It wasn't a Fortune Cookie idea as if God were only giving random promises of comfort or pleasant sayings to help people make it through a tough afternoon. It was a promise connected to a Story about a God who was different from the gods of Babylon and all the other gods of the world. It appeared for a time that these gods had won, and Israel often lamented their misfortune, suffering, and puzzlement as to why the pagan empires prevailed for centuries.

When Jesus started preaching *the Gospel of God* in Israel he was speaking to this condition of his people's enslavement and the enslavement of the world because it had rejected and replaced him with those things which were not gods. He was saying that the God of Israel was about to act to reverse this appearance of defeat. An "appearance" is all it was anyway. The gods of the nations were the ones that were weak, indifferent, and uncaring and God would come to

---

[39] Daniel 2:44-45

defeat those gods and vindicate his name. Because Israel was his people, *the good news of God* was the message of hope that the end to their suffering was at hand. God would deliver them. God would act and save them. God would come through for them and in the process reveal who he was to the world.

The Gospel of God, then, was a message for Israel and a message for every nation. God would save Israel, and through them bring salvation to the rebellious nations of the world. The world must turn from their idols and embrace the God of Israel, the true God. Thus, Paul wrote to encourage the Thessalonians who had turned from their idols with their false stories of empire and immortality to the one true God. They had embraced the Gospel of God. Paul wrote to the Romans that he was offering them as a sacrifice of worship to the one true God, now that they had turned from their pagan ways. When he was in Lystra and Athens, and presumably everywhere else, he exhorted the Gentiles to turn to the good news, the Gospel, of the world's true God and Lord.

How is this important for the challenges we face today? How does this emphasis equip and empower us?

Defeating Generic Theism

Earlier, I identified one of the great challenges the Church faces today – Generic Theism. The Church, like ancient Israel, has always faced the enemy of false gods. To ancient Israel they looked like the faces of Baal or Astarte, gods and goddesses of fertility or like the faces of Bel and Marduk, the gods of Babylon who had conquered Jerusalem. But the enemy has a different face today for it is telling its story in a new way. The new story is "your god is OK. My god is OK. Everyone's god is OK as long as we believe. Right?" And this is where we must humbly say, "No. Not right."

We live in a country where 94% of the people claim to believe in God. Big deal! In Paul's world, I would guess that 99.9999% of the people believed in God. An atheist was a rare commodity. The problem was that they believed in the wrong God, and the problem for us is that when people say they believe in God, they don't have a clue what they mean about "God," or, they have another version of God in their mind. This is why our message must include "the Gospel of God" – an explanation of who he is, his nature, his creative purposes, and his promises to restore the world to himself. When we do not present the Gospel of God to people, we may not be giving the proper theological context, worldview perspective, or narrative background for our presentation of the Gospel of Christ.

Today, the promotion of Generic Theism is in full swing. We hear of:

- The higher power of Alcoholics Anonymous
- The intelligent designer of academic debates
- The human-evolved-into-the-Father god of Mormonism
- The Great Mind or Soul of Hinduism
- The pantheistic god of new age spirituality

My guess is that these beliefs substantially pad the 94% of survey results. We no longer have the luxury of assuming that "God" means the God of the Bible to everyone. We certainly would not assume that in India. We should no longer assume it in the West. And for this reason, when we present the Gospel, we may first need to present the Gospel of God – the good news of who God is, what he is like, what he has done, and his call for absolute allegiance and solitary worship. We can illustrate it like this, the Gospel of God is the first of three components of the overall message of the Gospel.

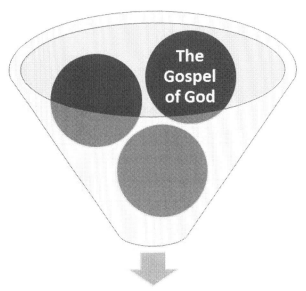

The Gospel of the True God vs. the False Gods of the World

If we do not present our Gospel within the context of the truth about God, our listeners may not understand who Christ is. What is the truth about God others need to know?

- He is the creator and is not part of creation.
- He interacts with his creation and reveals himself to the world and is not distant and aloof.
- He makes and keeps promises and is not capricious and unpredictable like the gods of mythology.
- He acted supremely in Christ – the ultimate and complete revelation of his character and plan.
- He is acting today in the proclamation of the good news to the nations.

- He will act in the future with further salvation[40] and judgment[41] to renew all things.

Remembering that Gospel means *good news* we proclaim these truths, not as dry, propositional, abstract theological statements but as good news for the hearers and as the true Story that supersedes and corrects all other stories! The true Story tells us that a holy, majestic, all-powerful, and caring God really does exist! We are not alone in the universe! He has spoken to us! He has come to us! Life and history have meaning! The future is certain, and we can have hope. To borrow a phrase from a great theologian and philosopher – *he is there and he is not silent!* [42]

Because there is no god like our God, because he is the only God, the whole world must forsake their idolatrous stories of empire and their paths to immortality. They must turn from whatever caricature of the true God they possess and embrace the true story and the true God in spirit and in truth. With Jesus and Paul, we must become heralds of the Gospel of God.

---

[40] 1 Thessalonians 1:10 – After explaining how the Thessalonians had turned from idols to the true and living God, Paul then said they were to wait for the Son from heaven who will rescue from the wrath to come.
[41] 1 Peter 4:17 – "For it is time for judgment to begin with the household of God; and if it begins with us first, what will be the outcome for those who do not obey the Gospel of God?" See also Revelation 14:6-7
[42] Francis A. Schaeffer, *He is There and He is not Silent*, Tyndale House Publishers, 1972.

Jonathan Williams

Chapter 4 – *The Gospel of the Kingdom*

AFTER MARK INTRODUCED JESUS' MINISTRY by saying that he was preaching the Gospel of God, he then quoted these words of Jesus, "The time is fulfilled and the kingdom of God is at hand. Repent and believe in the Gospel" (Mark 1:15).

The phrases "the time is fulfilled" and "the kingdom is at hand" make it clear that Jesus was connecting to a deep story line and that it was much more than abstract propositions about the nature and being of God. This storyline was the Gospel of the Kingdom of God. Matthew is more explicit, "Jesus was going throughout all Galilee, teaching in their synagogues and proclaiming the Gospel of the kingdom, and healing every kind of disease and every kind of sickness among the people," Matthew 4:23.

In Luke 16:16 Jesus stated, "The Law and the Prophets were proclaimed until John; since that time the Gospel of the kingdom of God has been preached, and everyone is forcing his way into it." The Gospels make it clear that the emphasis of Jesus' message was the Gospel of the Kingdom. Consider these statements he made about the kingdom.

- It is the basis for repentance. "Repent, for the Kingdom of heaven is at hand." – Matthew 4:17
- It is to be sought above all else. "But seek first His Kingdom...."– Matthew 6:33
- It is to be treasured above all else. "The Kingdom is like a treasure hidden in the field, which a man found and hid; and from joy over it he goes and sells all that he has...." – Matthew 13:44-46
- It has priority over all relationships and possessions. "Truly I say to you, there is no one who has left house or wife or brothers or parents or children, for the sake of the Kingdom of God...." – Luke 18:29
- Its mission is the most demanding and noble in which anyone can engage. "No one after putting his hand to the plow and looking back, is fit for the Kingdom of God." – Luke 9:62
- Its message was the theme for the "12 and the "70" in their ministries. "And as you go, preach, saying, 'The Kingdom of heaven is a hand.'" – Matthew 10:7 "And heal those in it who are sick, and say to them, 'The Kingdom of God has come near to you.'" – Luke 10:9
- It is the purpose for which Jesus came. "I must preach the Kingdom of God to other cities also, for I was sent for this purpose." – Luke 4:43

What is the Gospel of the Kingdom of God? This is an important question to answer. In another book,[43] I have shown that the four Gospels contain 110 references to God's kingdom. Of these 110 references, 101 are statements in the mouths of the main characters in the Gospels. Of these 101 statements, 94 are from the mouth of Christ. Obviously, the kingdom of God was an important topic to him!

---

[43] *God's Kingdom Plan*, Jonathan Williams, 1986, unpublished.

The Gospel of the Kingdom that Jesus proclaimed is the good news that the true God, the creator of all things, has begun to reign on earth as promised by the prophets of Israel. The word, *kingdom*, has the emphasis of *the exercise of kingly authority*. When John and Jesus announced that the kingdom was *at hand*, they were saying that God's reign on earth was imminent. This was good news because it would mean an end to the rebellious kingdoms of the world, salvation for God's covenant people, and salvation for the nations that would turn to him. The true Story would replace the false stories in the world.

But Jesus did more than announce that God's reign was imminent. He preached the good news that God's reign had come to earth. When, for example, he cast out a demon, he stated "the kingdom of God is upon you,"[44] he was announcing that God had inaugurated his kingly authority on earth and was exercising that authority by driving Satan out of people. When the Pharisees asked him when the kingdom was coming, Jesus answered, "The kingdom of God is in your midst!"[45] The problem that many had with Jesus' kingdom message is that it didn't look like the kingdom of their imagination.

Many fine Christians have thought that the kingdom of God was a message only for the Jewish people early in Jesus' ministry. After being rejected in the first part of his ministry, he abandoned his teaching on the Gospel of the kingdom to Israel and preached a more universal Gospel of grace. But this perspective is hard to maintain in light of the following points.

---

[44] Matthew 12:28 and Luke 11:20
[45] Luke 17:20-21

1. Jesus continued to speak of the kingdom all the way to the Cross.[46]
2. In the Olivet discourse, he stated that the Gospel of the kingdom would be preached to *all the nations*.[47] It was not just a message for the Jews.
3. After his resurrection, Luke characterized his 40 days of teaching in this way. He was speaking "of the things concerning the kingdom of God." (Acts 1:3)
4. Philip preached the kingdom of God to the Samaritans. (Acts 8:12)
5. Paul preached and taught it on his missionary journeys (Acts 14:22; 19:8; 20:25). In 20:25 he summarized his apostolic ministry as "preaching the kingdom" just a few breaths after he stated that he was preaching the Gospel of the grace of God (20:24). Obviously, the two were interchangeable in Paul's thinking, or the one Gospel presented from two angles – God's reign coming back to earth (kingdom) and God's sovereign initiative to reach out to a rebellious world in darkness (grace).
6. In Acts 28:31, Luke's last verse, he recorded Paul's preaching theme – "preaching the kingdom of God and teaching concerning the Lord Jesus Christ with all openness, unhindered."
7. Finally, the epistles contain 18 references to the kingdom of God, most of them in Paul's letters. It was

---

[46] See, for example, Matthew 21:31 in the parable of the Two Sons (21:28-32); Matthew 21:43 in the parable of the Vineyard; and Jesus' statement to Pilate in John 18:36.

[47] Matthew 24:14. Compare with Mark 13:10 where this is simply stated as *the Gospel* being preached to all the nations. Also, see Matthew 26:13 and Mark 14:9 where Jesus spoke of this Gospel being preached in the whole world. In the context of his last week, this can only be the Gospel of the kingdom of God.

a topic of Christian instruction and believers were to walk worthy of God's kingdom.[48]

The Gospel of the Kingdom, therefore, was not a temporary message for Israel. It was a message for all the nations. God did not want to rule in Israel alone, but in the whole world. After all, the whole world belonged to him! It is only logical to think that he would want to reclaim it. The means by which he would accomplish this was through his Messiah and his people. The mission of Jesus to Israel would become a mission of his followers to the nations. This is crucial to grasp if we are going to engage the challenges to the Gospel and change the stories of the world.

Fortune Cookie Christianity

Let's take a look at a second challenge I have identified, "Fortune Cookie Christianity" – the reduction of our faith to pious sayings, verses, and commands. Of course we want God's people to memorize verses and obey God's commands. But when God's people never learn to connect these to the storyline, they greatly reduce their opportunity to grow and to affect the world around them.

The Gospel of the Kingdom of God is a powerful remedy to this problem for it tells us that our Gospel connects to a world-wide and history-long story. The Story tells of a God who created a beautiful world and placed image bearers to live in it, to cultivate it, and to manage it for his glory. But the story took a dreadful turn. The image bearers rebelled against the King and in spite of his loving efforts to restore them, they continued to rebel and set up defiant kingdoms in the world and created offending caricatures of the true

---

[48] For example, Romans 14:17; 1 Corinthians 4:20; Colossians 1:13, 4:11; 1 Thessalonians 2:12; 2 Thessalonians 1:5; Revelation 1:6.

God. The world plunged into darkness. Yet, God continued to reach out to the world of men, promising through his people Israel that he would restore his reign upon the earth. Those rebels who submitted to his kingdom could find release from sin and the restoration of his image in them. God would create a people for his glory, and he would one day fill the earth with his glory – paradise would be restored.

The Gospel of the Kingdom of God is the Narrative of Power we are to tell the world. We are to preach and teach *God's reign on the earth and that every person must submit to his authority.* Here are the basic components of the Gospel of the Kingdom.

- God has come to the earth in Jesus Christ and has inaugurated His kingly rule. By no means am I suggesting that everything about the kingdom of God has been fulfilled but I am saying that the future reign of God when it will be completely manifested and when every enemy is beneath his feet *has started on the earth* through the person and work of Jesus Christ. One can see this in Luke 4:18-19 where Jesus grounded his miraculous ministry in Israel in the kingdom prophecies of Isaiah 61, saying that he fulfilled them. Jesus was not saying that everything in the Kingdom or every prophetic promise had been fulfilled at that moment, but that he had inaugurated the movement that would inevitably lead to its full presence on earth. Jesus' works of power were the first acts of God's reign on earth. The kingdom would not come all at once but in stages beginning with his ministry.
- Jesus inaugurated the kingdom through his sacrificial death. One thinks of the great passages in Revelation where John says that by his blood, he makes us to be

kings and priests (Revelation 1:5-6; 5:9-10). In his book, John says that the slain Lamb is the one who overcomes, opens the Book of Destiny (Revelation 5), and presides over history culminating in his glorious return when the kingdoms of the world become the kingdom of God and his Christ (Revelation 11:15).

- Jesus inaugurated the kingdom by his immortal resurrection. Paul in 1 Corinthians 15:20 calls Jesus the first fruits of the end-time resurrection of God's people. We can say that the end-time kingdom resurrection has started because the first of many people to be raised has been raised and glorified. Paul also has this thought in mind when he calls Jesus the firstborn from the dead in Colossians 1:18.

- Jesus inaugurated the kingdom with his enthronement to the right hand of God. In Acts 2:25-36; 13:32-37; Romans 1:1-4; Hebrews 1:5; 5:5; and Revelation 3:7, the various speakers and writers picture Jesus as the One who has fulfilled the Davidic promises spoken by the prophets for God to seat a son of David on the throne of Israel from which he would rule over the nations. *He reigns now* while the Father puts enemies beneath his feet (1 Corinthians 15:23-28).

- Jesus inaugurated the kingdom by his gift of the Spirit. In Acts 1:4-5, Jesus identified the next key moment of the kingdom for his disciples – the empowerment of the Holy Spirit – and in Acts 2 we see the bestowal of this gift and Peter identifying it as the fulfillment of Joel's prophecy of the Spirit for Israel. This gift empowered his people to take the kingdom message that had been preached in one nation to every nation.

This is the framework of the Great Commission and the preaching of the Gospel – the kingdom inaugurating events in Jesus' ministry, his death, resurrection, enthronement, and Spirit empowerment for his people. In this context of kingdom inaugurating events, he commissioned the apostles to preach the kingdom to the whole world and summon the nations to quit their rebellion and obey him.[49] One day the King will return, judge all men, heaven and earth will reunite, and his kingdom will perfectly manifest itself on earth. Paul expresses the climax of it all in 1 Corinthians 15:28 – "God will be all in all."

We are a long ways from "God loves you and has a wonderful plan for your life!" Although a true statement and one that God has used to introduce countless men and women to Christ, this popular evangelistic phrase is *a morsel* of the Gospel. Because it is true and its simplicity speaks deeply to the need for love, purpose, and release from sin, it is powerful and able to affect salvation. But again, this is only *a crumb* from the Master's table when he invites the Church, and the nations through the Church, to his Gospel *banquet*. Or, to use the Story metaphor, he invites us to explore, learn, and tell the full story and not just a portion of it. We are part of a history-long, world-wide story! When God's people learn and embrace this Story, the Narrative of Power – The Kingdom of God – they will find themselves letting go of Fortune Cookie Christianity for something far greater.

The Gospel of God tells us good news about the true God, what he is like, and that he interacts in a gracious way with his creation. The Gospel of the Kingdom of God tells us specifically what this God has done in the world to reestablish his kingdom authority and make all things new. The Gospel of the Kingdom becomes the second component alongside the Gospel of God and we illustrate it in this way

---

[49] Notice Paul's emphasis of the Gentiles obeying in Romans 1:5 and 16:26. See also 1 Peter 1:2.

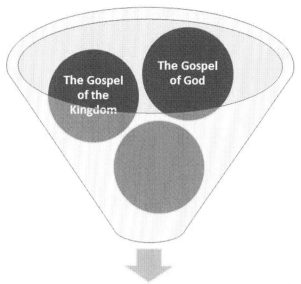

**The Gospel of the True God and the
Kingdom vs. the False Gods
and Empires of the World**

We have now created the proper theological context, worldview perspective, and storyline for our presentation of the Gospel of Christ. The Gospel of Christ will tell us who God worked through to inaugurate the kingdom and who will complete the kingdom mission. This is the next chapter and a crucial component in the Narrative of Power. We must add this piece and connect it with the other two if we are going to change the stories of the world.

Jonathan Williams

Chapter 5 – *The Gospel of our Lord Jesus Christ*

THE GOSPEL OF OUR LORD JESUS CHRIST is by far the most popular expression of the Gospel and some combination of these words is the most widely used in the New Testament, apart from the simple phrase, *the Gospel*. It is not hard to understand why. In Jesus Christ, the God whom no man can see became visible. People saw him, touched him, heard him, and told others to come and see. He walked the earth. He reached out in compassion to the sick and the sinners. He performed miraculous deeds, he died for the sins of the world, he rose three days later, he ascended back to heaven where he was enthroned as Lord of all, poured out the Spirit to empower his followers to spread the good news, and now sits at the right hand of the True Power waiting until every enemy is put beneath his feet.[50] It is all about *him*!

God's people will hold to these truths without question. Yet to maintain the centrality of Jesus Christ, some will push back against what I have said so far about the Gospel of God

---

[50] Psalm 110:1; 1 Corinthians 15:27-28; Hebrews 10:12-13

and the Gospel of the Kingdom. Perhaps, as you have read, questions have been raised in your mind.

I have had good, veteran, godly pastors say to me, "What do you mean the Gospel of God?" Or, "The Gospel of the Kingdom? Wasn't that a message for the Jews in the first century and a message for them in the future?" Or, "Are you trying to add something to the pure, simple Gospel message? Are you trying to add works to grace?"

I'm not making this up. Pastors have reacted to the things I have said fearing that I was undermining the necessity of the death and resurrection of Jesus Christ. "The Kingdom of God! Are you pushing a secret agenda of Dominion theology where we are expected to take over the world?"

And then, as if to prove their point about the pure, simple Gospel message we are to hold to, the message of Jesus Christ, they point to 1 Corinthians 15:1-4 with its beautiful and classic description of the Gospel we all love.

> Now I make known to you, brethren, the Gospel which I preached to you, which also you received, in which also you stand, by which also you are saved, if you hold fast the word which I preached to you, unless you believed in vain. For I delivered to you as of first importance what I also received, that Christ died for our sins according to the Scriptures, and that He was buried, and that He was raised on the third day according to the Scriptures.[51]

"That settles it," they say. "The Gospel is the death, burial, and resurrection of Christ – nothing more. Here it is in black and white."

But does that settle it?

---

[51] 1 Corinthians 15:1-4

Understanding the Gospel in 1 Corinthians 15

Let me make two observations about this passage we all love that will hopefully clarify this confusion. First, Paul said that Christ died for our sins *according to the Scriptures*. By this, we all understand that the Old Testament spoke of his death. We quickly open our Bibles to Isaiah 53 and read the moving words of the Servant bearing the iniquity of his people. But Paul also said that the Christ would rise *on the third day according to the Scriptures*. Where in the Old Testament does it say that the Messiah will rise from the dead on the third day? You will be looking a long time because no verse says it.

We do find two passages where something amazing happened on the third day. We know the story of a runaway prophet, thrown into the sea, swallowed by a great fish, and regurgitated on the third day. Amazing – like a resurrection from the dead. Most of you know I am talking about Jonah, the story Jesus used to illustrate his death and resurrection and vindicate his claims to Messiahship.[52] Jesus would be swallowed up, not by a great fish, but by death itself. He would die and be buried and then just like Jonah would emerge from his tomb on the third day.

Here's another story – the ministry of Hosea to sinful Israel. Among his prophecies is a lament about the sinfulness of the people of God in Hosea 5:1ff. God had warned them, repeatedly, but they continued in their wicked ways leaving God no choice but to judge them. God is described as a lion who tears and badly wounds the people. But the people know that this judgment from God is to teach them an important lesson. In a beautiful song of praise they say that God will come to them and raise them up on the third day. He will bring healing to them that they may live before him.

---

[52] See Matthew 12:38-40.

¹ Come, let us return to the Lord. For He has torn us, but He will heal us; He has wounded us, but He will bandage us. ² "He will revive us after two days; He will raise us up on the third day, that we may live before Him. ³ "So let us know, let us press on to know the Lord. His going forth is as certain as the dawn; and He will come to us like the rain, like the spring rain watering the earth.

The people would be ripped and wounded but raised on the third day. The prophet was swallowed and returned to life on the third day. In the story of Jesus Christ we find the fulfillment of these stories. The ultimate prophet was swallowed by something far worse than a great fish and brought back to the world of men on the third day. In the story of Jesus Christ we find an innocent, sinless one bearing the sins of the people, being wounded and bruised for them and then being revived, resurrected, made alive by God on the third day. These two stories, and perhaps others, Paul had in mind when he wrote that the Scriptures said the Messiah must be raised on the third day.

Where am I headed with this? What is my point? My point is that the resurrection of Christ *on the third day according to the Scriptures* can only be verified within the context of the story of the Creator God (the Good News of God) who was working within his people Israel to restore his kingdom (the Good News of the Kingdom) on earth.

1 Corinthians 15:3-4 is not a stand-alone two or three point outline detached from everything else that happened in the working of God's plan in the world and among his people.[53]

---

[53] Theologians use the term synecdoche which means a part that represents a whole. For example, the phrase, "The Law and the Prophets" often refers to the entire Old Testament. Darrell L. Bock, research professor of New Testament Studies at Dallas Theological Seminary says, "…only to speak of Jesus dying for sin – even to speak of

Right here in the heart of Paul's explanation of the Gospel we have evidence that Paul was drawing from the larger story to give texture and deeper meaning to the story of Christ's death and resurrection. Christ rising on the third day was not an incidental fact as if he could have risen on the second day or fourth. He had to rise on the third day because that is how the Story was being told. God did great things for people in distress on the third day.[54]

A second observation on 1 Corinthians 15 is this: has anyone noticed that verse 4 does not end with a period, but a comma? Yes, we know Greek did not have punctuation and we are free to put a period there if we wish, but the next verse begins with the word "and". Paul's Gospel presentation does not end in verse 4 but continues. Look at it again. No one would think of putting a period after verse 3. Why do we do it (not literally, but logically) after verse 4?

> [3] For I delivered to you as of first importance what I also received, that Christ died for our sins according to the Scriptures, [4] **AND** that He was buried, **AND** that He was raised on the third day according to the Scriptures, [5] **AND** that He appeared to Cephas, then to the twelve.

Jesus dying for sin *and* rising again – is to give only about half of the gospel message," *Recovering the Real Lost Gospel*, p. 3.

[54] G.R. Beasley-Murray agrees that Paul's and Jesus' third day wording "almost certainly implies a reference to Hosea 6:3." He elaborates on this by saying "Hosea 6:3 is but part of a body of literature in Judaism in which note is taken of God's acts on the third day. In the Midrash on Genesis 42:17 there is a famous comment, 'The Holy One, blessed be He, never leaves the righteous in distress more than three days.'" He then provides a lengthy quote from the Midrash Rabbah emphasizing *third day deliverances* within the history of Israel. With this mindset in God's covenant people, it makes perfect sense why Jesus would emphasize a *third day resurrection* for it would be the day of His deliverance and vindication from God. See *Jesus and the Kingdom of God*, Beasley-Murray, p. 246-47.

For Paul, the resurrection appearances are part of the Gospel. That was part of his message and presentation just as with Peter in Acts 3:14-15 and 10:40-42.

> 14 But you disowned the Holy and Righteous One and asked for a murderer to be granted to you, 15 but put to death the Prince of life, the one whom God raised from the dead, a fact to which we are witnesses.

> 40 God raised Him up on the third day and granted that He become visible, 41 not to all the people, but to witnesses who were chosen beforehand by God, that is, to us who ate and drank with Him after He arose from the dead. 42 And He ordered us to preach to the people, and solemnly to testify that this is the One who has been appointed by God as Judge of the living and the dead.

In verses 5-11 Paul is doing the same thing as Peter as he lists the people who saw the resurrected Jesus. Then in 12-19 he elaborated on the importance of the resurrection. He explains that it is proof that what happened to Jesus on the cross was to save us from our sins. If there is no resurrection – there is no substitutionary death. If there is no resurrection, Jesus was only another would-be Messiah and his death was just a tragedy. But with the resurrection we learn that the death of Jesus was the triumph of the Kingdom.

Then, in verse 20 Paul places the resurrection back within the story by tying the resurrection of Jesus to the Adam story and showing how Jesus is the Man who reverses the curses the first man brought into the world. This new Man is now enthroned at the right hand of God and reigns. All enemies are being placed beneath his feet and the kingdom is being restored. The process that will lead to the restoration of all things that Adam lost was inaugurated in Jesus' death and resurrection and continues up to our day as Jesus reigns from the right hand of God. One day that reign will be completed and God will be all in all.

Paul's Gospel explanation, therefore, is not verses 3-4 only. The Gospel is not just the death and resurrection of Christ but also his enthronement and ultimate defeat of all enemies in order to restore all things. Salvation is not just being forgiven so we can go to heaven when we die. Salvation is the full restoration of God's reign over all things, and Jesus Christ (the Gospel of our Lord Jesus Christ) is the means by which the true God (the Gospel of God) restores his kingdom (the Gospel of the Kingdom) in his creation. We can now complete our illustration begun two chapters ago when we spoke of the Gospel of God.

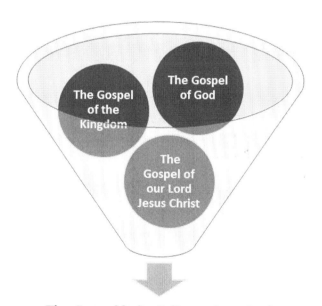

**The Gospel in its Fullness Preached
to the Nations of the World**

Apostolic Preaching

Connecting the Gospel of Christ with the Gospel of the Kingdom and the Gospel of God brings other Scriptures into focus. Notice Philip's twofold message to the Samaritans.

> But when they believed Philip preaching the good news about the kingdom of God and the name of Jesus Christ, they were being baptized, men and women alike. – Acts 8:12

The two parts of Philip's message were the Gospel of the Kingdom of God and the name of Jesus Christ. How do they work together? Philip was announcing God's reign on earth, summoning the Samaritans to the obedience of the God of Israel and telling them the means by which they could enter his kingdom – the name of Jesus Christ. The person and work of Jesus Christ is the means by which sinners can re-enter the reign of God that man rejected through sin.

Paul's preaching in Asia carried the same twofold emphasis.

> But I do not consider my life of any account as dear to myself, so that I may finish my course and the ministry which I received from the Lord Jesus, to testify solemnly of the Gospel of the grace of God. And now, behold, I know that all of you, among whom I went about preaching the kingdom, will no longer see my face. – Acts 20:24-25

This passage is part of Paul's farewell address to the elders in Ephesus and contains a summary of his message to them and others. Paul stated that he preached the Gospel of the grace of God. Then, in his next breath, he mentioned that he preached the kingdom of God. God's grace through Jesus Christ in his death, resurrection, enthronement, and return to consummate all things is the means by which the kingdom is restored and God becomes all in all. These are not two Gospels but one Gospel. As Paul went through the cities of the Roman Empire to Jew and Gentile, he preached

God's kingdom and the means by which people could enter the kingdom – the grace of the Lord Jesus Christ.

Luke provided the same emphasis when he concluded his book and described Paul's ministry in Rome.

> When they had set a day for Paul, they came to him at his lodging in large numbers; and he was explaining to them by solemnly testifying about the kingdom of God and trying to persuade them concerning Jesus, from both the Law of Moses and from the Prophets, from morning until evening.
>
> And he stayed two full years in his rented quarters and was welcoming all who came to him, preaching the kingdom of God and teaching concerning the Lord Jesus Christ with all openness, unhindered. – Acts 28:23, 30-31

Notice in the final two verses that Paul preached and taught. His preaching was heralding, like a runner breathlessly arriving in a city with good news about a faraway battle that the city's king has won. Paul came to city after city in the ancient world to tell them that the true king of the world had won the victory for mankind. Then he taught them how he had won it – by teaching them about the Lord Jesus Christ.

This is why the kingdom *of God* in the Gospels and Acts has become the kingdom *of Christ* in the epistles. Christ is the means by which God establishes his reign on earth among men. And because Jesus is Lord, we can rightfully call it his kingdom. All authority in heaven and on earth is his.

> For this you know with certainty, that no immoral or impure person or covetous man, who is an idolater, has an inheritance in the kingdom of Christ and God. – Ephesians 5:5
>
> For He rescued us from the domain of darkness, and transferred us to the kingdom of His beloved Son. – Colossians 1:13

I solemnly charge you in the presence of God and of Christ Jesus, who is to judge the living and the dead, and by His appearing and His kingdom. – 2 Timothy 4:1

For in this way the entrance into the eternal kingdom of our Lord and Savior Jesus Christ will be abundantly supplied to you. – 2 Peter 1:11

Then the seventh angel sounded; and there were loud voices in heaven, saying, "The kingdom of the world has become the kingdom of our Lord and of His Christ; and He will reign forever and ever." – Revelation 11:15

Then I heard a loud voice in heaven, saying, "Now the salvation, and the power, and the kingdom of our God and the authority of His Christ have come, for the accuser of our brethren has been thrown down, he who accuses them before our God day and night. – Revelation 12:10

God's people can now rightfully call the Kingdom of God *the Kingdom of Christ* because of what he has done. This is why the Gospel in the New Testament is commonly called *the Gospel of Christ*. It is the good news that the God of creation has sent his anointed one, the Christ, to inaugurate his kingdom and bring salvation to the world.

Some verses call it the Gospel of *Jesus* Christ because they identify who the promised Christ is. He is Jesus of Nazareth. Some verses call it the Gospel of *the Lord* Jesus Christ because Messiah Jesus has been raised from the dead and exalted as Lord over all. Some verses call it the Gospel of *his Son* because the Lord Jesus Christ is the Davidic Son, fulfilling the promises to David.[55]

---

[55] Many references to Jesus as the Son of God are not references to His being the second person of the Trinity. Instead, they refer to Him as the Davidic Son of God. For example, when the Father said, "this is My beloved Son in whom I am well pleased," He was not saying, "This is

But whichever combination of words we use, it is important that we put the story of Jesus Christ within the larger framework of the Gospel of God and the Gospel of the Kingdom. It is important in order to get the story correct and important to help us engage challenges in our world. We have already talked about the challenges of Generic Theism and Fortune Cookie Christianity. It's time to look at a third challenge – The Mystic Messiah.

Engaging the Mystic Messiah

A third challenge the church faces today is one that relativizes the uniqueness of Jesus and reduces him to a mystic like other mystics and teachers of "timeless truths." We have combated this spirit of syncretism by quoting a few key verses:

- I am the way, the truth, and the life, no one comes to the Father but by Me (John 14:6).
- And there is salvation in no one else; for there is no other name under heaven that has been given among men by which we must be saved (Acts 4:12)
- For there is one God and one mediator between God and men, the Man Christ Jesus (1 Timothy 2:5).

These are great words and potent weapons. But let me suggest a far more powerful weapon – the weapon of connecting the story of Christ to the greater story of the Gospel of God and the Gospel of the Kingdom. Let me explain.

Why should we believe, for example, the *Gospel of John* over the *Gospel of Thomas* or the *Gospel of Mary Magdalene*? Today,

---

My Son, the Second Person of the Trinity." Instead, He was quoting Psalm 2, which prophesied that the Davidic Son would rule the world.

many advocate giving equal weight to them all and speak of the different versions of Christianity in the ancient world. If one Gospel is as good as another, why would John 14:6 take precedent over a verse, say, in *Thomas*?

Here is how we answer this question. We ask, "which Gospel connects to the Narrative of Power in a cohesive way? Which Gospel completes the story begun in the Good News of God and the Good News of the Kingdom? Does Thomas complete the story? Does Luke? John? Which ones?"

When one examines the *Gospel of Thomas*, one discovers there is no narrative at all! It is just a collection of sayings; some identical to the traditional Gospel statements, some roughly similar, and some completely different. But because *Thomas* has no narrative, one can take a "Jesus saying" and place it within whatever framework he likes to tell whatever story he likes! Actually, the sayings in *Thomas* do tell a story of sorts, or, at least provide a perspective, but it is not Christian. It is a Gnostic work providing a strange conclusion to a centuries long story that was headed in another direction.

This is more apparent in the *Gospels of Mary Magdalene* and *Philip*. The *Gospel of Mary Magdalene* provides some narrative, but when we examine it, we discover that it is telling another story – the Gnostic story – which has a different approach to life, a different worldview, and a different destiny than the controlling narrative of Scripture – the kingdom of God. Imagine telling your children the story of the three pigs as you tuck them into bed at night. You build up the storyline and you get to the climax of the big bad wolf trying to blow down the house of bricks, but as you do so, you suddenly start telling the story of Jack and the Beanstalk. He climbs down the beanstalk with the giant chasing him and the giant steps on the house smashing it to pieces and the wolf, who turns out to be hero, gobbles up the selfish pigs. You start with one storyline but end with another. Your kids would look at you and say, "What are you doing? You are messing up the story!"

The other Gospels so many hear about today are doing exactly that – they are messing up the Story! When we understand the sayings and events in the life of Jesus within the Gospel of God and the Gospel of the kingdom of God, we put it in its right context and have a bulwark against the spirit of syncretism that relativizes Jesus. Failure to put the Gospel of Christ within the larger Storyline of the Kingdom of God opens us to dire consequences.

Without the overarching Story, we can more easily reduce Christ to another religious teacher with timeless words of wisdom about the mystery of life. The uniqueness of his message and identity are lost. Without the Story, we can synchronize Christ's words with eastern religions or incorporate them into other religious tales that present a vastly different view of reality, the purpose of life, and how people return to God. But with the Story, we can confidently affirm the biblical Gospels over today's trendy embrace of these other Gospels that tell a different tale.

Our culture of tolerance and syncretism will exact a great price of us to maintain the truth of the Gospel of Jesus Christ, but maintain it we must, even at the cost of our lives. While we wish and work for tolerance and peace among all religions, we must also persistently, persuasively, and faithfully hold up the uniqueness of Jesus among men. He is not another founder of a religion among many other religions and their founders. He is the Consummation of the true Story of the world. And while many try to blend the similarities of all religions into a substance suitable to the tastes of everyone, we must insist that there are elements of all religions that are not blend-able with others – and especially the story of Jesus. He is unique for only he fulfilled the Story of God that had been unfolding for centuries.[56]

Another reason exists why we must place the story of Christ within the larger story of the Kingdom – many reduce the Gospel to an outline and a transaction. The outline is that God loves us, we are sinners, Jesus died for us, he rose again, we believe in him, and we go to heaven when we die. The transaction is, "pray this prayer." And although these facts are true and God hears our prayers, the Gospel is much more than an outline and a transaction.

Imagine someone telling us about Tolkien's novel, *The Lord of the Rings*. We have heard that it is one of the greatest works of fiction ever created. We are excited, ready to read it but when they bring it to us, all we get is a Cliff Notes version. "This is it?" we ask. We read it, and though we get the gist of the story, somehow it doesn't come across as glorious as we have heard. Or imagine someone telling us about the classic movie *Ben Hur* and his struggle with Messala which was a microcosm of Israel's struggle with Rome. We are excited to watch it but all we receive is a trailer, a preview.

Unfortunately, this is what the Gospel is for too many Christians and non-Christians. It is an outline of a few key points – a Cliff Notes version, a trailer of the greatest story and drama known to man. It is something to acknowledge in some kind of prayer and then people go on their way to life

---

[56] We are doing what ancient Israel did – shine a light in the darkness of the world of paganism. Ancient Israel persisted in its faith that their God was the true God. They would not compromise with paganism, and they resisted efforts to blend with other ancient religions. For this, they were looked down upon and considered atheists by the society at large, although also protected by Roman law from having to sacrifice to Caesar. But they maintained that their God was the true God and their Story the true story.

as normal. They have failed to connect with the Greater Story of the Gospel of God and the Gospel of the Kingdom.

God has much more for his people. An outline and the transaction are useful. But the Gospel is a story. It is the Story about the greatest person in the universe – the Creator who is powerful, beautiful, holy, and full of love. It is his Story about his plans for the earth and every person in it, a Story about an unthinkable act of rebellion and selfishness that has caused untold pain and suffering for everyone. It is a Story of a Hero who suffered unimaginably in order to rescue the people that he loves. It is a Story of his plans to restore the kingdom on the earth.

In separating the outline and transaction from the Story and Drama the Bible painstakingly tells, we open ourselves up to other dangers.

- Without the Story, the transaction becomes mere fire insurance. Believe, escape Hell, and Heaven awaits us when we die. But what happened to the summoning of the nations to obedience of faith – or, as Paul put it to King Agrippa – *performing deeds appropriate to repentance?*[57] What happened to the gathering into a community like-minded people with a heart of love and service to shine light into the darkness?
- Without the Story, the Gospel becomes an "other-worldly" matter instead of the story of this earth and the rightful King reclaiming what is his. Justice on earth loses its importance in view of this "other worldly" emphasis and the development of personal piety. We erode the basis for obedience and living a holy life on this earth, and what holy living there is often is a matter of adhering to rules instead of kingdom obedience.

---

[57] Acts 26:20

The Gospel of God, the Gospel of the Kingdom of God, and the Gospel of the Lord Jesus Christ who revealed the true God and inaugurated the kingdom – they are the same Gospel, different ways of looking at the one message with which God has entrusted us for preaching and teaching. Understanding the Gospel in all these dimensions equips us to engage the challenges that face the church today and empowers us to live a life of obedience to the king. If we are going to change the narratives of people and nations, we must equip ourselves with the Narrative of Power, the narrative that is more compelling and exciting than all the stories of the world.

Chapter 6 – *The Apostles, God's Storytellers*

WE HAVE A GREAT PRIVILEGE as inheritors of the Gospel message, the message to which prophets pointed, Jesus inaugurated, and apostles proclaimed. But a trap lies hidden in the shadows – the assumption that we share the Gospel with the same framework as the apostles. Let me explore this for a moment.

In the West, especially, we share the Gospel in a highly individualized way. Nothing is wrong with that for each person is precious to God. We see Philip one-on-one with the Ethiopian on the Gaza road preaching Jesus to him. Ultimately, every person must make up his mind, make an individual choice for or against Christ. But often we put this choice in a way that is disconnected from the Story of Scripture. In some respects, this is understandable because many people have very little knowledge of the Old Testament background to the Story. Also, we often share the Gospel from a "sinner-in-need-of-forgiveness" angle and certainly nothing is wrong with that!

But we would benefit greatly by examining how the apostles connected their Gospel presentation with the Story of Scripture. We noted in Acts 8:35 that when Philip preached Jesus to the Ethiopian on the Gaza road he did so *beginning* from Isaiah 53. *Beginning*, that's an important word for it implies that it was only the start of Philip's presentation, and he likely had many other Old Testament points of reference to share the full story with the Ethiopian, even if he only had the scroll of Isaiah.

When Paul climaxed his message in Pisidian Antioch with a word about forgiveness of sins,[58] we discover that he spoke about freedom from the Law of Moses and finished with a quotation from Habakkuk. His presentation was not a simple, bare-bones outline that we are accustomed to sharing with people; "God loves you, you sinned, sin brings death, Christ died for your sins, pray this prayer and receive his forgiveness so you will go to heaven when you die."

I am not saying these points are wrong, and outlines can be helpful. But we must remember what outlines are and their purpose – tools to aid us in recalling the content that they represent. I suggest that we devote ourselves to learn more than an outline of a Gospel presentation and that we train God's people to fill in those outlines with the Bigger Story they represent.

In this chapter, I wish to focus on an important but often overlooked characteristic of apostolic evangelism; connecting their Gospel presentation with the Larger Story. If Isaiah 53 was *the beginning* of Philip's presentation of Jesus, he must have confidently shared the entire story of Jesus within the framework of the Story his people had been telling for centuries, i.e., the Gospel of God and the Gospel of the Kingdom. When Paul preached forgiveness to the Jews

---

[58] Acts 13:38

in Pisidian Antioch, he framed it within the greater story of Israel's purpose, failure, and hoped for deliverance that would also bring deliverance to the nations. We start in this chapter by examining the apostles as "storytellers," with Paul's message to the Jews recorded in Acts 13.

Paul's Message in Acts 13

In his message, Paul used a descriptor of the Gospel that we listed in Chapter 3 – *the Gospel of the promise made to the fathers*. We find it in 13:32 where Paul said,

> We preach to you *the good news of the promise made to the fathers*.

What is the significance of this phrase? Its significance lies in Paul's tying his message to the story of Abraham, Isaac, Jacob, and other great "fathers of Israel" to whom God made promises. It shows the apostles as storytellers for when they preached, they connected their Gospel message of Jesus to the Story that had been developing for centuries. They built a framework for their message about Jesus. We would do well to study their method and imitate it for the audiences to whom we speak. Let's break down Paul's message and notice what he did.

1. The message begins in 13:17 and we discover that we must read six verses before we find any reference to Jesus. Paul mentions God's election of Israel, their stay in Egypt, the Exodus, the wilderness wandering, and their settling in Canaan. He then jumps to Samuel the prophet, Saul the king, and the raising up of David, a man after God's heart who performed God's will. Why does Paul do this? – because of the emphasis he wants to place on Jesus as the Son of David. Later in his message he also tied in to the hope

of every Jew that the great son of David would come and bring deliverance. But in order to present Jesus this way, he must first present the historical framework.

2. In 13:23, he finally mentions Jesus and proclaims him as Israel's Savior. But that's all he says at this point and it is only a teaser for more that is to come.

3. After mentioning Jesus, Paul backtracks and speaks of the ministry of John for two verses in 13:24-25 emphasizing that John's purpose was to point to a person so amazing that he was not even worthy to loosen the sandals of his feet.

4. With this background, Paul then presents the heart of his message, and he starts it in 13:26 with the announcement that God is sending the message of salvation to the Jewish people – the announcement they had been waiting to hear for centuries. Remember the idea behind the concept, Gospel, we examined in Chapter 2, the concept of a runner announcing good news to a city? This is what Paul is doing in his ministry.

5. *Then he preaches Jesus* starting in 13:27. He begins with the events that caused so many Jews to stumble – his death. A crucified Messiah doesn't sound like the promised Son of David. But Paul ties the events of his death with prophetic Scriptures, key components of the Story that had been unfolding for centuries and that were now coming to pass in their lifetime.

6. Paul then comes to the great climax of his message (13:30ff) – God raised Jesus from the dead. Jesus appeared to many people and appointed them to be witnesses of his resurrection to the people. But what is the significance of the resurrection? – in the fact that it is the fulfillment of the promises and the climax of the Story God had been unfolding for his people for

centuries. This is where Paul makes his bold statement:

We preach to you *the good news of the promise made to the fathers.*

7. Paul then fills in the meaning of the resurrection of Jesus by listing what these promises were and by saying the salvation God promised Israel had come! Listen to his words in 13:32-37

> [32]And we preach to you the good news of the promise made to the fathers, [33]that God has fulfilled this promise to our children in that He raised up Jesus, as it is also written in the second Psalm, "you are My Son; today I have begotten you." [34]As for the fact that He raised Him up from the dead, no longer to return to decay, He has spoken in this way: "I will give you the holy and sure blessings of David." [35]Therefore He also says in another Psalm, "You will not allow Your Holy One to undergo decay." [36]"For David, after he had served the purpose of God in his own generation, fell asleep, and was laid among his fathers and underwent decay; [37]but He whom God raised did not undergo decay.

Paul presented Jesus in the context of the Story of God worked out in the history of Israel. No outline here. No individualistic message only here, but a story for a people that had reached its climax in the life, death, and resurrection of Jesus.

Paul connected his message to a narrative that had been unfolding for thousands of years. It was not a new message of abstract truth about God and how to follow nice, moral platitudes from an impressive new teacher in Israel. Nor was he simply trying to get people into heaven at some future date. Instead, he was stating that the Story God had been telling through his spokesmen for centuries had taken a major turn!

This major turn is the point of the prophecies that Paul used. Paul is not proof-texting, merely showing how Jesus fulfilled a few references in the Old Testament. Instead, he is quoting from Psalm 2, Psalm 16, and Isaiah 54, all passages written by David, about David, or David's son who was destined to rule the world. God raised Jesus from the dead (Psalm 16) and enthroned him (Psalm 2) in fulfillment of the prophecies about David ruling the world (Isaiah 55).

Each of these passages (especially Psalm 2 and Isaiah 55) are telling a story of how God would use a special person in Israel's history to bless Israel and the world through Israel. Paul says that time of blessing has come. The promises made to the Old Testament men of God are now in fulfillment mode. Blessing is pouring from the throne of God to Israel and the nations of the world – the very hope of Old Testament prophets. The forgiveness of sins that Israel hoped for was now in their grasp. Their sins had caused their exile which continued even after some had come back to the land. But with forgiveness through Jesus, their exile was over and they could find freedom from the condemning Law of God that could only point out the nation's sin. Then, Paul warned the people that they should not scoff at this new work God was doing in their day. If they did, they would miss the Messianic blessing promised to them for ages.

Grinding a Theological Axe?

Am I just grinding a theological axe and advancing an obscure theological agenda? Or can we see that Paul's Gospel message about Jesus' death and resurrection was rooted in the Gospel of God and the Gospel of the Kingdom? When we grasp Paul's perspective and the method he used to address his people, we can equip ourselves with a perspective that can strengthen us to overcome the challenges we have already mentioned – Generic Theism, Fortune Cookie Christianity, and the Mystic Messiah. In connecting our Gospel to the history-long story of the Gospel of the Kingdom, we learn that the Gospel is not merely an existentialist, timeless message to individuals who hear it one-by-one who then, after they die, go to heaven one-by-one to live an eternal spiritual existence unrelated to earth. The Gospel is much more than a string of verses that we connect to convince sinners to repent. The Gospel is a story about the true God, his plan for our world, and the One who perfectly executed that plan in the world for the sake of the world.

Where is the reference in Paul's presentation about "going to heaven when we die?" You will not find it. Of course, we do go to heaven when we die, but that's not the point of the Gospel! The point of the Gospel was and is to bring blessing to Israel and every nation of the world and to summon the nations to obey the resurrected and enthroned King who is the promised Son of David who will one day make all things new.

The message of "receive Jesus and you will go to heaven when you die," while true, is closer to the heresy of Gnosticism that the church battled for centuries than to apostolic preaching *if it is divorced from the Great Story*! Again, the goal is not to go to heaven! The goal is to bring the blessing of heaven to all the nations through apostolic preaching with the goal of renewing the earth through that preaching and through the return of Jesus Christ.

Could this be one of the reasons why our churches are plagued with a consumerism mind-set rather than a heart of service and love? The Gospel we so often preach is all about *them*! But the Gospel the apostles preached called people to repentance and to forsake their false gods and stories, to embrace a new life of obedience, and to join the community of the people of God where they were to love and serve one another for the glory of God.

The Gospel of the Kingdom creates the theological foundation for community and the priority to love one another. God has not merely saved us from Hell so that we can go to Heaven when we die, he has saved *a people* for himself[59] who are to love one another and display his glory on earth. The ancient community of Israel understood this as did the generation to whom Paul preached. It is important for us to understand it also.

The Gospel of the Kingdom of God shows us that the Gospel is not about *us*. It is about *him*! The Gospel of the Kingdom is a history-long, "this world" story of God's involvement with the rebellious race of Adam, his covenant with the people of Abraham, and his efforts to use them to restore to the world what it lost through sin. The goal is for him to reveal his glory perfectly on earth as it is in heaven and for his image bearers to enter into the life of peace and joy he intended for them from the beginning. The Gospel, from this perspective, matches our definition of the nature of God as both transcendent and personal. He is eternal and above creation, yet he involves himself with his creation and has a plan he is working out in the world.

Perhaps, if we understood fully the story of the Gospel of the Kingdom of God, and how Jesus came to finish one part of the story for one nation in order to take it to a world-wide level for all the nations as he promised to Abraham,[60] we

---

[59] Titus 2:14 – Who gave Himself for us to redeem us from every lawless deed, and to purify for Himself a people for His own possession, zealous for good deeds.

[60] In Galatians 3, Paul grounds his apostolic ministry to the Gentiles in the promise to Abraham that all the nations would be blessed in him.

would preach and teach with greater authority in our summoning rebellious sinners to repentance and the obedience of faith. Notice how Paul preached to King Agrippa. We would do well to follow his example.

> So, King Agrippa, I did not prove disobedient to the heavenly vision, but kept declaring both to those of Damascus first, and also at Jerusalem and then throughout all the region of Judea, and even to the Gentiles, that they should repent and turn to God, performing deeds appropriate to repentance.[61]

We see Peter preaching with the same emphasis in Acts 2. He connects everything to the Story. He first connects the events of Pentecost with the promised pouring out of the Spirit in the prophet Joel. He then speaks of Jesus' death and then throws in that greatly significant word – BUT. "You nailed him to a cross ... BUT ... God raised him from the dead." Peter then explains the significance of the resurrection in 2:25-36, God fulfilled the promises to seat a son of David on the throne. Jesus is that Son of David and he is Lord and Christ, therefore repent!

What if Our Listeners Don't Know the Story?

But how do you preach to those who do not have the background of the Story? We can understand Peter and Paul preaching this way to the Jews steeped in their history, holding on to their promises, and hoping for their fulfillment. But what about people who know nothing of this Story? Do we have to give them a survey of Old Testament history before we can preach Jesus to them?

Many of God's people are discovering that providing a framework, a narrative, is extremely helpful. A good friend of mine serves in a part of the world with his wife where

---

[61] Acts 26:19-20

people do not know the Old Testament story. But he has found great success in telling the story of Christ, by beginning with the story of creation. Many have seen the amazing video of the missionary who went into Papua New Guinea and did the same among the Mouk people.[62] After learning the language, he told the story of creation and then the story of the Old Testament leading to the story of Christ. The villagers were riveted with these tales and when they heard that Jesus was killed they mourned deeply. When they heard he rose from the dead they erupted in joy. When they heard they could now have forgiveness, that Jesus was the fulfillment of the promises, the Lord of all, the entire tribe believed at one time.

Luke gives a hint in Acts 14 and 17 of how the apostles spoke to people without the background as he records Paul approaching those without a background in God's works throughout the history of Israel. In 14:14-17, in Lystra, he starts with the Gospel of God. He talks about God's creation, humanity, idolatry, and the worship of the one true God. In times past, God let the nations go their own way with the implication that it was time for them to turn from going their own way and go "God's way." This is conversion and this is repentance. In Acts 17, Paul elaborates on these themes and then declares that God has overlooked the times of ignorance and now declares to all men to repent of their idolatry and embrace the God of creation. The reason is that God will one day judge the world through a person that he raised from the dead. As you can see, Paul was emphasizing the Gospel of God instead of the Gospel of the Kingdom but the goal was the same, submission to the King of the world.[63] And we can assume that once people did turn from

---

[62] You can find this amazing story, Ee-Taow, at http://usa.ntm.org/ mission-videos-and-mission-photos.

[63] See also Acts 17:6-7 where these men have upset the world because they were proclaiming a lord besides Caesar.

their idols to the true God, his discipleship program would include filling them in on the rest of the story, the Gospel of the Kingdom.[64]

Paul's Benediction

We turn now to one more section in Scripture to reinforce our point. This is not a sermon but a closing benediction in Paul's letter to the Romans.

> [25]Now to Him who is able to establish you according to my Gospel and the preaching of Jesus Christ, according to the revelation of the mystery which has been kept secret for long ages past, [26]but now is manifested, and by the Scriptures of the prophets, according to the commandment of the eternal God, has been made known to all the nations, leading to the obedience of the faith. [27]To the only wise God, through Jesus Christ, be the glory forever. Amen.[65]

Starting with the end of the passage and working to its beginning, we discover this:

1. **16:27** – The goal of everything is to bring glory to the only God (the Gospel of God) through Jesus Christ (the Gospel of Jesus Christ). This matches Paul's explanation of the Gospel in 1 Corinthians 15 where the goal of the death, burial, and resurrection of Christ (the Gospel of our Lord Jesus Christ), and his enthronement (the Gospel of the Kingdom) is that the kingdom be given back to God so that he may be all in all (the Gospel of God).

---

[64] It is also helpful to realize that just as the Gospel of Christ is encased within the bigger story of the Gospel of the Kingdom which is encased within the bigger story of the Gospel of God, in the same way, the history of Israel is encased within the bigger of story of the history of mankind.

[65] Romans 16:25-27

2. **16:26** – The objective of Paul's preaching was to bring nations into the obedience that comes through faith in Jesus the Messiah. Paul phrases it this way, – *My Gospel ... according to the commandment of the eternal God, has been made known to all the nations, leading to obedience.* It is noteworthy that Paul also began his letter in this way. "We have received grace and apostleship to bring about the obedience of faith among all the Gentiles…" (Romans 1:5).

3. **16:26** – Paul's preaching was not a "new" message for a "new age" unrelated to what God had been doing in the past. It was the goal toward which God had been working for centuries through Israel. *My Gospel ... is manifested ... by the Scriptures of the prophets.* Paul's Gospel is the explication of Old Testament prophecies. Paul is saying much more than "Jesus fulfilled prophecies." He is saying that his Gospel and his apostolic preaching are grounded in the Old Testament narrative and advance the kingdom story.[66]

4. **16:25-26** – *The revelation of the mystery ... is manifested.* For centuries, the Jews struggled to understand how all the prophecies would work out. But in the life, death, resurrection, and enthronement of Jesus, God now reveals the mystery. God now commands that this message of how he fulfilled the story go to all the nations so that the nations could obey in faith. What his Son preached in one nation, Israel, God expands to all the nations through the preaching of the followers of his Son.

Once again we see how the apostles always connected their

---

[66] Paul also does this in Romans 10:15 where he bases his apostolic preaching in the Gospel of the Kingdom proclaimed in Isaiah 52:7. In 15:20-21 he grounds it in the Suffering Servant song of Isaiah 52:15 and claims that his mission work is what the prophets were speaking about.

preaching, their teaching, their praying, and their words of benediction with the Bigger Story, and we would do well to learn how to do the same for people in our day. We must do it for the lost, telling them a powerful story that is greater and more compelling than any story they know. We must do it for those in the Church, advancing their discipleship by helping them learn the full Story and connect their lives to it for God is calling them to be key players in his Story for the world. This will equip our brothers and sisters to resist the "Messalas" in their lives who seduce them and lure them away with an inferior and wrong story.

In our preaching of the Gospel in all its dimensions, therefore, we are telling people the incredibly good news that the creator of the world has acted within his creation in kind, providential ways, and he has acted in specific, concrete, gracious ways, in fulfillment of promises made long ago to reestablish his kingdom on *this planet*. The emphasis of the Gospel of the Kingdom is that God has begun to reign on earth and is summoning everyone to submit to the crucified, risen, and enthroned King with humility and gratitude. "Turn from your sins, receive his pardon, be filled with his Spirit, live in obedience, and spread the good news as you wait for the Son to return!"

With this perspective, we can see how the Gospel of the Kingdom of God carries with it a "this-world" emphasis. If we die before he returns, we will go to heaven. Yes, of course! But heaven is only a resting place on the way to the final destination – our resurrection when God manifests his perfect reign on earth. In 1 Thessalonians 4:13-14, we find that those who die before Jesus returns are safe with him. Jesus taught his disciples to pray, "Your will be done on earth as it is done in heaven." God has always manifested his kingdom perfectly in heaven. His goal is to manifest it perfectly on earth, the realm he created for man to live.[67] This will occur through Gospel preaching and his return.[68] When he returns he will bring them with him! In the Book of Revelation, the New Jerusalem comes down out of heaven to the new earth. One day, after God subjects every enemy to the feet of Christ, he will then display the full measure of his kingdom for his people to see and enjoy, all to his glory. God will be all in all.

---

[67] The heavens are the heavens of the Lord, but the earth He has given to the sons of men. – Psalm 115:16

[68] I am not advocating any sequence of end-time events. I am merely saying that the God who inaugurated the kingdom through Jesus Christ advances it through apostolic preaching and will consummate it when He sends the King back.

Chapter 7 – *Replacing the Stories of the World With the Superior Story*

W E COME NOW, TO THE GOAL OF THIS BOOK, changing the stories of the world with the superior story, the true story that we call the Gospel. How can we do this with wisdom and with power? First, let's answer the question we posed in Chapter 2, "What is the Gospel?" I would like, first, to provide a full description of the Gospel.

The Gospel is the good news of God – a message about the one true God of the universe and the earth. It is good news about who he is and what he has done. The Gospel is the good news of the kingdom of God; he is re-establishing his reign on this earth and has acted decisively to inaugurate it through Jesus Christ and to spread it to the ends of the earth through his covenant people. The Gospel is the good news of the Lord Jesus Christ. Jesus of Nazareth is the promised Christ and through his perfect life, substitutionary death, immortal resurrection, authoritative enthronement, and life-giving Spirit – all in fulfillment of the Scriptures – he has opened the door to immortality so that men can escape judgment and re-enter the kingdom that he originally created mankind to enjoy.

Now, I will shorten this description to something more like a definition and answer the question, "What is the Gospel?"

> *The Gospel is the good news about*
> *the nature of the one true God who created everything,*
> *His saving activity to re-establish his kingdom on earth,*
> *and the One through whom he accomplished this*
> *kingdom salvation – Jesus Christ.*[69]

I'm sure you can see the three components of the Gospel in this definition – the Gospel of God, the Gospel of the Kingdom, and the Gospel of the Lord Jesus Christ – and how they work together.

All are needed to speak to the multiplex, deep needs of people today. The Gospel of God is needed to release people from their idols, whether they be idols of wood, stone, or any created thing which we place in the center of our lives.

---

[69] We could also add to this definition the phrase *and the means by which we enter His kingdom and receive salvation – faith.* But our response to the Gospel is not the purpose of this book and for that reason I did not include it.

Every person has an instinctive reflex to worship something. Jesus told the woman of Sychar that it was important to worship in spirit and in truth. People must abandon their false gods or false ideas of god and embrace the one true God. God is seeking worshippers.

The Gospel of the Kingdom is needed because every person on the planet is in rebellion. Some are overtly in rebellion. Others more subtly so and may not even be aware of it, but every person's sin is an act of lawlessness and God is calling all men to repent of their lawlessness, their rebellion and submit to his reign in their lives. Both Paul and Peter spoke of bringing the lost into obedience to the King. Every person has a control reflex in their lives. At some level they wish to control their lives, their destiny. They must give control of their lives to the Lord of heaven and earth.

The Gospel of the Lord Jesus Christ is needed because every person has a guilt reflex which causes him to hide or relieve his guilt in some way. Jesus offers the only way to find relief from guilt and condemnation and enter into peace with God. The Gospel of the Lord Jesus Christ is needed because every person needs to see that salvation is by grace. It is not by our efforts, our achievements, or our goodness. Jesus was God incarnate revealing himself to the world and showing the world how it must live in submission to his authority. He also died for the sins of the world to take away the guilt of all mankind. Only through the crucified, risen, enthroned Lord can people return to the kingdom of the one true God.

All dimensions of the Gospel are needed to speak to these deep reflexes and instincts in all of us to worship, to control, and to assuage guilt. But now that we know these three dimensions of the Gospel and see how they connect, how do we present the Gospel in all these dimensions to those who have been believing and living a different story? How do we change the stories of the world?

First, we must recognize two levels of story in the world. I call these micro stories and macro stories. Micro stories are the small stories people live by. They are personal and they relate to their life experiences, the choices they have made, and the values by which they live. Macro stories are the big stories that control families, communities, people groups, and nations. Most people in the world are connected to some type of macro story and most people live a mixture of the two. First, let's look at the micro stories people experience.

Micro Stories

Everyone has a story, and it is always a jumble of many events, experiences, and choices. Usually one or two micro stories will rise to a place of prominence and shape a person's life.

Most stories involve some type of significance issue. By this, I mean that people live for some type of goal or purpose. I have discovered four of them. They are:

1. Possessions – people focus on acquiring the necessary things of life. Nothing, of course is wrong with this. But often, the story takes a strange twist and people start living for the accumulation of possessions and become controlled by the desire to have more. Their status and well-being is determined by the amount of their possessions.

2. Power – people focus on getting ahead of others. Again, this does not have to be wrong. Some people are natural leaders with a highly competitive nature. But the twist comes when getting ahead means putting others down. In its worst form, some people become tyrants. It may be tyranny in the home or tyranny of a nation.

3. Pleasure – people focus on the enjoyment of life. God has given us all things to enjoy. He is a God of pleasure and he created us to enjoy the pleasures of his creation. The twist in this story is when people place the enjoyment of created things above pleasing God. Created things become central and people become swallowed up by a never- ending thirst for a new pleasure. Some aspect of creation, rather than the Creator, becomes central to their lives.

4. Prestige – people want to be known, affirmed, valued, and recognized, and like the others, this does not have to be sinful. But people often cross a boundary where legitimate relationships and affirmation descend a steep slope to an abyss with a never ending hunger for attention.

Everyone has a mixture of these four drives. How we go about fulfilling them creates the values and shapes the story by which we live. People can fulfill these natural drives in a God-pleasing way, or they can fulfill them in selfish, illegitimate ways, sinful ways. Their story becomes twisted and complex with consequences that bring pain, confusion, and a search for a remedy for the pain and confusion. As people search they turn to a thousand different stories in the world that promise relief and a reorientation of life that will bring wholeness. Most of the stories in the world are false, a mixture of truth and error, or incomplete. Only one Story is completely true and brings lasting significance.

In addition to the developing Significance stories that come from choices and drives, many people also live out what I call Wound Stories. Wound stories come from the consequences of the wrong things others do to us. The wrong things could be words or actions. The words parents say to children penetrate deeply into their small souls and fill them with poisonous lies – feelings of unworthiness, shame, worthlessness, or contamination. Often, these feelings will rise to a place of domination over a person's personality and will highly influence the choices a person makes and the direction a person takes in life. Sometimes, people experience unspeakable atrocities that set them on a course that results in a sad, painful tale. Just as with the Significance stories, people seek for relief from the misery of their wounds and they can turn to a thousand different remedies that promise help. Only one remedy, only one Story can bring complete healing.

Every person is a jumble of significance stories gone bad and Wound stories. Layer upon layer of stories covers them. Sometimes people are only faintly aware that they are living these stories. Many are like fish in the ocean that are not aware of the water in which they swim. Some have lived within their stories for so long they may now take them for granted and believe them to be the reality they must live by or the "true story" for their lives. I believe this is what Ephesians 2:1-3 is about.

> [1] And you were dead in your trespasses and sins, [2] in which you formerly walked according to the course of this world, according to the prince of the power of the air, of the spirit that is now working in the sons of disobedience. Among them we too all formerly lived in the lusts of our flesh, indulging the desires of the flesh and of the mind, and were [3] by nature children of wrath, even as the rest.

The triumph of the false story seems complete in the lives of people as described in this passage. We live by the false stories of our misguided and out of control desires which are reinforced by the culture of this world and behind it all is a manipulative, powerful spiritual entity that weaves a destructive web of lies appealing to a person's desire for significance or healing from a wound. Sometimes, people live in them so long that they have made an uneasy peace with their web of lies and trudge through life as best as they can.

Then, we come to them with the Gospel. What is our mission? It is to cut through the layers of their false stories with a different Story. This is where it is important to equip ourselves with more than an outline about how people get to heaven when they die. We must know the full story of the Gospel of God – the story of the creator, his character, his intentions for people, our waywardness, our idolatries, and his restoring love.

We must know the story of the Gospel of the Kingdom – this creator has acted in kingly, royal ways to rescue people and the whole world from the false Significance stories and Wound stories. We must know the story of the Gospel of the Lord Jesus Christ – the One who embodies the Creator in flesh and who carries out God's royal purposes for people and the world. When we equip ourselves with the Larger Story, we can with great wisdom, untangle the knots that bind people as we apply the different dimensions of the Gospel to the different parts of their experience. I think you can see from these scenarios that resorting too quickly to the outline and transaction may be a mistake. Although, it will become appropriate at some point, our task is to intersect a person's false story with the True Story and lead them out of their web of lies into the freedom that God provides. And we can do so with confidence as we realize that God's Spirit is already mightily working in a person's life cutting through the web of lies and laying them open and ready to receive the life giving message of Jesus.

Macro Stories

Most people in the world also live by Macro stories. Macros stories are the large stories that weld people into communities, tribes, and nations. They dominate a culture so thoroughly that even a highly individualized culture, like the West, can have a certain way of thinking that influences and shapes every person. Our own culture in the United States is shaped by many Macro stories including the Gospel although that story is in decline and is being replaced by others. Here are three Macro stories that are wielding great influence in the world today.

1. The Secular Story – this story says that everyone's religion or faith is OK, as long as they keep it private and to themselves. They must never impose, in any way, their views upon others. The reason for this is that all religions are matters of faith and opinion and not rooted in empirical knowledge. They are incapable of being proven by scientific measures and one grasps them only by a "leap of faith." This does not mean they are invalid or even wrong but only that one's story has just as much validity as another's. What is true for you may not be true for me, and vice versa. Therefore, while I am happy that you have "a truth", I have my own which probably differs from yours, and we'll just all agree to disagree and keep our faith private. We will leave matters of government and social ills to the political and social leaders who make their policy decision from the facts of science and reality.

2. The Mysticism Story – this story finds fertile ground in the Secular Story. If religion is a private matter with little to no bearing on society, then the best form of religion is the eastern form where a person discovers his link with an other-worldly divine force. A person need not attend highly structured religious communities because the goal is not a social goal but only a personal one. The goal is not the restructuring of earth but the escape from earth to ascend to higher

levels of spirituality in "heavenly realms" be this "heaven," "nirvana," or some kind of "astral plane." The goal is the full realization of one's own divinity and the merging of the person into the great Oneness of the divine. Buddhism, Hinduism, and New Age beliefs are different ways of advancing this story in the world.

3. The Islam Story – this story can, strangely, cut across the grain of the first two, because of its concreteness. People grow tired of too much privatization and mysticism and look for something that has order and discipline for this world. Islam presents itself as the solution for this world's problems and as the culmination of God's great story. The one true God, the creator of the heavens and the earth has always spoken through prophets. His next to last prophet was Jesus and the final prophet is Mohammed who spoke the ultimate words of God for the world. All should heed these words, submit to Allah, and perform the five pillars of Islam. One day the entire world will become Muslim.

One may wish to present other Macro stories, but I believe these are sufficient to express my main point – most of the world finds itself embracing one of these stories. Today, 1.5 billion are Muslims and billions more hold to a form of mysticism, and at least hundreds of millions have bought into the Secular Story.

When we add a Macro story on top of every person's micro stories which are a jumble of Significance stories goes astray and Wound stories that penetrate deeply, we discover that people can be highly complex. This may leave us feeling overwhelmed. We may ask "Who can be saved?" But this is our task – to change the narratives of the world, and I hope you can see that we must equip ourselves with far more than an outline and a transaction about how people can go to heaven when they die. If this is all we have, we are attempting to scale mountains in gym shorts and tennis shoes. If this all we have, we are laying siege to castle walls with small caliber weapons. We need cannons, big cannons, and I would suggest that the big cannons come from understanding the three-fold dimension of the Gospel which places the story of Christ within the larger stories of the Kingdom of God and the Gospel of God.

Again, such a task can feel overwhelming. It feels that way because it is that way. But this is why Paul asked believers to pray for him in the preaching of his gospel, that he would make it clear to people.

> Devote yourselves to prayer, keeping alert in it with an attitude of thanksgiving; praying at the same time for us as well, that God will open up to us a door for the word, so that we may speak forth the mystery of Christ, for which I have also been imprisoned; that I may make it clear in the way I ought to speak.[70]

This is why Paul's statement in Romans 1:16 is so powerful – I am not ashamed of the Gospel because it is *the power of God* for salvation. God's Story is more powerful than any other story in the world, and when we learn to present it humbly, clearly, and with the power of the Holy Spirit, we will find our Story penetrating and replacing the false micro stories and macro stories in which people find themselves. This is why Jesus told the apostles, "you will receive power to be my witnesses to the ends of the earth." And we can take great comfort from the words of Jesus. After he said it is easier for a camel to go through the eye of a needle than for a rich man to enter the kingdom of God, Peter asked, "Then, Lord, who can be saved?" And Jesus replied, "With men,

---

[70] Colossians 4:2-4

this is impossible, but with God all things are possible."

God loves the world and he intends for the world to hear his Story. He said he would be with us and that he would give us the power of the Holy Spirit. He also commissioned us to go into all the world and to make disciples, which implies that we can change the stories of people by his grace.

Preaching and Teaching the Gospel

Because people come to Christ from many motivations and with different levels of understanding, it is our duty to know the full Gospel and to train our churches in it. The reasons are twofold: first, we must help our people conform their entire story into the full story of God, his kingdom, and his Christ. Second, in doing so, we equip them to free others still caught in the webs of the world. Teaching someone how to share the Bridge Illustration is a good and useful exercise. Every Christian should know it. But how much better if we can educate every Christian with the Narrative of Scripture and train them on how to apply it to others.

We often hear about *preaching* the Gospel, but we do not hear much about *teaching* the Gospel. We must continually teach our church the good news of God, the good news of the kingdom, and the good news of all that Jesus Christ has done. This does not mean giving message after message on John 3:16. The apostles wrote their letters to churches at various stages of maturity and growth. Some were full of brand new Christians, like the church at Thessalonica. Others were more established, such as the churches at Rome and Corinth. Great portions of their letters are explications of the Gospel, and by this I am not referring only to the apostles' efforts to show the believers how to live out the Gospel. I mean that great sections of their letters were explanations of what the Gospel is. We could look at the entire book of Romans this way. Paul began 1 Corinthians 15 with this statement: "Now I make known to you brethren, the Gospel...." Did they not already know the Gospel? Well, yes and no. They knew enough to know that Jesus Christ was the way out of the darkness of the world. But much of the Gospel remained for them to learn, piece together in a coherent way, and apply to their thinking and their living.

This is discipleship. We never leave the topic of the Gospel! Our mission is not to preach the Gospel and then teach something else. No, we are to preach *and teach the Gospel*.[71] Everything must flow from the good news of God, his Kingdom, and his Christ. When we learn to do this, tangents, irrelevant issues, and heresies will diminish. They will have a harder time taking root in the heart of a Christian that has been cultivated and nourished with all the dimensions of the Gospel. Christians will become healthier and more effective in presenting the message to a world that is full of wrong stories, a world that needs to have its narratives change.

The outline of the Gospel that we so often share works fine when it is the thin edge of a wedge. But for too many of us, our presentation remains only a thin edge with insufficient power to open the person fully to the glory of our God. But knowing the full Gospel, the Gospel of God, his Kingdom, and his Christ enables us to insert the thin edge, push, and as the wedge broadens with more truth, the person's defenses will open and expose themselves to the greatness of our God who reigns through Jesus Christ.

How much of the Gospel do people need in order to find

---

[71] Just like Jesus did as he went through Israel preaching (heralding) and teaching the kingdom. See Matthew 4:23; 9:35 where both are mentioned. See Matthew 13:54; Mark 1:21; 6:2; 10:1; Luke 4:15; 6:6 and 13;10 *for teaching* and Matthew 24:14; Mark 1:14; Luke 4:43; 8:1; 16:16 *for preaching*.

salvation? They must know enough truth about themselves to know they are in need and enough truth about him to know that only he can meet that need because of what he has already done for them through Jesus Christ. People don't know all about themselves when they come to Christ. Nor do they know all about him. But what they know of themselves and of him must be true. People cannot come to Christ if they are prideful and think they are capable of achieving salvation through a good life or self-help improvement techniques. Pride is a lie and shields them from the truth about themselves – they are sinners.

Nor can people find Christ's saving power if they think he is only a good teacher. Such falsehoods shield people from the light of who he is and what he has done through his life, death, resurrection, and enthronement. When people come to Christ, they must come to him in truth – in truth about themselves and him. The work of the Spirit of God upon a man is mysterious. Only he knows when enough truth about Christ will penetrate a soul and bring humility, faith, and salvation.

The blind man in John 9 did not know much except that Christ made him see. "All I know is that I was blind and now I see." We must take people where they are and lead them to Christ according to their needs, not our agenda. Christ is sovereign and he knows the moment of faith in every person's heart. In Acts 10, Peter was not finished with his sermon, perhaps not even with his introduction, when the Holy Spirit came upon the Gentiles!

Christ is powerful. The Syrophoenician woman stated that she only needed a crumb from his table. Her daughter was healed. The bleeding woman touched the hem of his garment and was cured. The man in John 9 knew only that he was blind and then he saw. For people today, Christ acts with such power. Some carry a load of guilt. They hear of forgiveness, what Christ did for them on the cross, and find release and salvation. Others are empty and looking for more. They hear of the power of Christ in his life, death, and resurrection. They hear that he is Lord and they submit to him. Have these people heard all of the good news? Most likely not, but they have heard enough to come to him and in coming to him, they can now discover the full story that will be consistent with what they have already learned. They can hear *the rest of the story*!

These are the greatest acts of love in which we can engage for our non-Christian and Christian friends –

- to *preach* to them the Gospel in all its dimensions so that they will come to faith. This is the work of evangelism.
- to *teach* them the Gospel in all its dimensions so that they will grow in their faith. This is the work of discipleship.

End Times or Cultural Disintegration?

The Gospel – it is the most important story for our world, the Story the world desperately needs to hear. We can trace every problem in the world back to a wrong story about God, about people, about the purpose of life, about the destiny of the world, about how to overcome guilt and death. Our task is to change the wrong stories of our friends and the wrong stories *of the world.* The narratives that need changing are not personal only but sometimes family-wide, community-wide, nation-wide, and world-wide.

History shows us that in some places and at some times, the Gospel has not only changed scattered individuals, but it has shaken nations and shaped cultures. We who live in the West live in a culture profoundly shaped by men and women who took the Gospel beyond their personal lives and applied it to wider issues of society and culture. The definition of a family, of marriage, and the role and limitation of government are only a few of the many God-given structures of society the Narrative of Scripture has shaped. We are also seeing before our eyes what can happen when Powers separate these structures from the True Story and attach them to other stories. Culture – separated from Truth – disintegrates just as individuals who believe and live lies experience a slow death.

Many believe that the disintegration of our culture is a sign of the end times and that Jesus will soon return. I hope they are right! I want Jesus who inaugurated the kingdom to return and consummate the kingdom on earth! Yet, they may not be right, and the decline of civilization may instead be the effect caused by the rejection of the True Story at widespread personal and institutional levels. God may be calling his people, again, to a long range project of preaching the Gospel of the Kingdom that will penetrate multitudes of people so thoroughly that they apply their Gospel to every dimension of their lives and culture. Isn't that what some people call revival and reformation?

What could happen to the poverty of India, for example, if the Gospel took hold of the masses and if the implications of the Lordship of Christ extended to the cultural framework of that society – a framework that has enslaved hundreds of millions for centuries? What could happen in the Middle East if the Gospel penetrated so thoroughly that Jew and Arab embraced the way of Jesus? What if they gave "the land" back to its rightful owner – the Creator – and followed Jesus on the path of the cross, the path of humility, peace, and service? History would change – again! History has changed through the centuries because God's people dared to believe, follow, and preach the Gospel in all its dimensions. They changed the narrative of the culture in which they lived. Because God has chosen not to reveal to us the times and epochs of "the end" which he has set by his own authority[72] shouldn't we minimize speculation about end time details? And should we not instead set our hearts on the one thing he has revealed to us – "you shall receive power when the Holy Spirit comes upon you and you shall be my witnesses to the uttermost parts of the earth?"[73]

Only God knows how history will unfold and only the naïve or proud think they can figure it all out. We should leave that to God and set our hearts to do what he told us. If Jesus returns tomorrow, hallelujah! But if he does not, we must work to change the narratives of people and of the world for his glory in his world. We must take every thought, every philosophy, every worldview, and every story captive to the obedience of Christ. Is this not what Paul had in mind in 2 Corinthians 10:4-5 when he said,

> For the weapons of our warfare are not of the flesh, but divinely powerful for the destruction of fortresses. We are destroying speculations and every lofty things raised up against the knowledge of God, and we are taking every thought captive to the obedience of Christ.

We would also be naïve to think that the task will be easy. Not every person will greet our story with joy and wonder. Not every culture will greet it warmly. The lessons of church history show individuals and entire societies vehemently opposing it. In many places, especially places outside the individualistic, self-centered West, a person's personal story interweaves tightly with a family story, a tribal story, or a national/religious story. Just think of the trauma that a Hindu or Muslim often undergoes as he realizes the true

---

[72] Acts 1:7
[73] Acts 1:8

God is calling his entire substructure of reality into question! The Gospel brings people to a crossroads. Actually, the Gospel brings people to a cross they must bear – deny yourself, your past, your former life, and your ambitions. Forsake all, pick up your cross, and follow Me. Jesus called us to lose our lives for his sake and for the sake of the Gospel.

But in spite of opposition, we must faithfully preserve, preach, and teach the Narrative of Scripture to those who will listen. Our hearts must burn with passion for the Story and we must humbly but with confidence call people to repent of their false stories and embrace the truth. Paul was a man who sacrificed everything to take the biblical narrative to as many as he could for as long as God gave him strength. He said, "For I am not ashamed of the Gospel, for it is the power of God for salvation to everyone who believes, to the Jew first and also to the Greek."[74] May our hearts burn with such passion! When they do, we will find power to overcome the challenges that threaten the Church, we will faithfully advance the Kingdom, and we will bring much glory to our God in the world as we wait for the Son to return and consummate the Kingdom so that God may be all in all.

~~~

The Roman tribune Messala tried to lure his childhood friend Judah Ben Hur to accept the story of Roman glory and domination. But Judah Ben Hur refused and the battle was on. Messala struck first, imprisoning Judah's family and consigning Judah to slavery as a rower on a Roman battleship. But as we know, the tables were turned. In a miraculous turn of events, Judah became a hero in war, escaped slavery, rose to prominence, returned to his country

---

[74] Romans 1:16

as Messala's equal, and won the great chariot race that turned out to be Messala's death.

But a greater battle had to be won – the battle within Judah's heart which was in danger of becoming corrupt and self-serving like Messala's. It seemed his heart was destined to be yet another chapter in a long, worldwide story of bitterness and revenge, until he met the crucified Christ and found the story of his people strangely completed in one who did not take revenge but who forgave those who oppressed him. Judah's heart was released from its pain, his family was restored, and the river of water mixed with the blood of Christ that poured from the cross flowed into the world to change the stories of the world in order to make all things new for those who will believe.

The Greater Story

THROUGHOUT THIS BOOK I HAVE EMPHASIZED the importance of sharing the Gospel as a story within the greater story of God. I have chided, hopefully in a gentle way, the evangelical tendency to present the Gospel as an outline. Yet, it is useful to have a summary of the Gospel story and to know how to present it in a succinct fashion. What is the Greater Story in which we play a role? Like a good play, it consists of several Acts.

> *Act 1 – Creation*
> *Act 2 – Catastrophe*
> *Act 3 – Covenants*
> *Act 4 – Christ*
> *Act 5 – Commission*
> *Act 6 – Consummation*

Act 1 – Creation tells about the Creator. He is the all-powerful God. He is One. No other God exists. He makes all things to express his majesty and beauty including humanity. Humanity is the pinnacle of his creation. God made man and woman in his image to reflect his character. They are to be creative in their fulfilling of the amazing destiny he gives them – to manage and rule the earth for his glory and for the good of all mankind.[75]

Act 2 – Catastrophe introduces sadness into the Story. Something goes terribly wrong in Paradise. The man and woman turn away from the Creator. In an unthinkable act, they rebel against God and seek to establish their own authority. They introduce sin into the world, and its consequences – suffering, sorrow, and death – follow close

---

[75] Read about this in Genesis 1-2.

behind. As they bear children and their children multiply throughout the earth, the consequences of the rebellion cannot be shaken off and spread to all mankind.[76]

Act 3 – Covenants introduces a new figure in the drama. His name is Abraham. The Creator makes a covenant with him and promises blessings climaxing in the greatest blessing of all – through his descendants One will come who will rescue humanity from its rebellion and death. The descendants of Abraham become the nation, Israel. Israel is a light in the dark world. It exists to point the nations to the true God – the Creator of the universe. But Israel fails in its mission. It becomes like the other rebellious nations of the world and must be judged. Israel's prophets tell of this judgment, but they also tell of One who will come and restore the nation to its purpose and bring restoration to all mankind. He will bring salvation to the ends of the earth.[77]

Act 4 – Christ is the turning point in the Story. The Promised One comes! His name is Jesus. He takes the Story to a new and dramatic level. He lives among his people with humility and grace. He heals the sick, gives sight to the blind, and raises the dead. He sets free the oppressed, forgives sin, and tells stories of God's great love. Not everyone is happy with his mission. The political authorities are threatened. The religious authorities are suspicious and finally cannot condone his mission because it does not match their ideas of what the Deliverer will do. They conspire to arrest and try him. They crucify him for the crimes of blasphemy and revolution. Three days later, he rises from the dead, gathers

---

[76] Read about this in Genesis 3-11.

[77] Read about **the covenant with Abraham** in Genesis 12 and 15. You can find his entire story in Genesis 12-25. Read about **the covenant with Israel** in Exodus 19-20. You can read Israel's story in the Old Testament, Exodus through Malachi.

his followers, and prepares them for Act 5.[78]

Act 5 – Commission is when the resurrected Jesus commands his followers to go into the world and tell everyone the good news. The promise that God made to Abraham that he would bless the entire world will now come to pass because the Promised One has come. He lived among us. He died for our sins. He rose from the dead and is enthroned as the Lord of all. He gives his Spirit to empower his people to spread the joyful news that God will forgive all our sins. God and humanity can be reconciled. The original destiny God gave mankind, to display his image and to rule the world for his glory, can now be restored.[79]

This good news has now come as far as you! What will you do with it? The most famous verse in the Bible, John 3:16, says:

> *For God so loved the world*
> *that he gave his only begotten Son,*
> *that whoever believes in him shall not perish*
> *but have eternal life.*

Act 6 – Consummation is when Jesus returns and judges the world. Every person will give an account for his life. Every knee will bow and confess that Jesus is Lord of all and the only Savior of the world. Those who receive him will enter into eternal life. Those who do not will be separated from his love. The great goal of God's creation is for all rebellion to cease, for God to display his glorious kindness in the world,

---

[78] Read about Jesus in the Gospels of the New Testament – Matthew, Mark, Luke, and John.

[79] You can find the Great Commission in these verses: Matthew 28:18-20; Mark 16:15-16; Luke 24:44-49; John 20:21; and Acts 1:8. You can read about the first efforts to proclaim the good news in the world in the Book of Acts.

and for all things to be made new.[80]

God wants every person to receive his love and to be part of the Greater Story. He also wants every person to bring the good news to others. Have you received this life-restoring message and become part of the Story? Are you telling it to others?

We would like to hear from you and encourage you. If you have received Christ as your Savior or if you have taken a significant step to become involved in God's Greater Story, write and tell us your story. You can write us at:

Word of God, Speak
PO Box 90047
San Antonio, TX 78209

Reach us on the web at www.WGSministries.org or email us at info@WGSministries.org. We look forward to hearing from you!

---

[80] You can read a quick overview of the end in 1 Corinthians 15:20-28 and Revelation 20-22.

Appendix A – *The Gospel*

This appendix and the ones that follow can help you in your study of the Gospel as revealed in the New Testament. I have looked up all references in the New Testament where the nouns "Gospel" (from the noun *euangelion*) and "Good News" (from the verb, *euangelizo*) are used and categorized them into the following categories:

- The Gospel
- The Gospel of God
- The Gospel of the Kingdom
- The Gospel of Jesus Christ (or a similar designation)
- Other designations for the Gospel

Throughout I have made a few comments on the verses and to connect verses in one category of the Gospel with another. You will know this by the highlight.

This appendix focuses on New Testament references which speak only of "The Gospel." You will find 73 verses which use only "The Gospel." However, the context and comparison with parallel passages will show that many of these are references to the Gospel of the Kingdom and to the Gospel of God. Some of the passages are contextually rich showing how all components of the Gospel work together.

Matthew 11:5 – The blind receive sight and the lame walk, the lepers are cleansed and the deaf hear, the dead are raised up, and the poor have the gospel preached to them.

This verse contains phrases from Isaiah 35:5 (the blind receive sight) and 61:1 (the poor have the Gospel preached to them). Because of the contexts of those two passages, they should be interpreted as Gospel of the Kingdom verses. See also Luke 7:22.

Matthew 26:13 – "Truly I say to you, wherever this gospel is preached in the whole world, what this woman has done will also be spoken of in memory of her."

This statement followed close on Jesus' statement that the Gospel of the Kingdom would be preached in the whole world (24:14). The similarity in terminology "preached in the whole world" indicates that he had in mind the Gospel of the Kingdom in this verse. See also Mark 13:10.

Mark 1:15 – And saying, "The time is fulfilled, and the kingdom of God is at hand; repent and believe in the gospel."

It should be clear that the good news Jesus was bringing was good news of the coming reign of God. "The kingdom is at hand. Repent and believe this good news!"

Mark 13:10 – The gospel must first be preached to all the nations.

Luke 7:22 – And He answered and said to them, "Go and report to John what you have seen and heard: the blind receive sight, the lame walk, the lepers are cleansed, and the deaf hear, the dead are raised up, the poor have the gospel preached to them."

Mark 14:9 – "Truly I say to you, wherever the gospel is preached in the whole world, what this woman has done will also be spoken of in memory of her."

Mark 16:15 – And He said to them, "Go into all the world and preach the gospel to all creation."

Luke 1:19 – The angel answered and said to him, "I am Gabriel, who stands in the presence of God, and I have been sent to speak to you and to bring you this good news."

Good news is used here in more of a generic sense of a

wonderful message being given by Gabriel to John that he would have a son.

Luke 2:10 – But the angel said to them, "Do not be afraid; for behold, I bring you good news of great joy which will be for all the people."

Luke 3:18 – So with many other exhortations he preached the gospel to the people.

Luke 4:18 – "The Spirit of the Lord is upon me, because he anointed me to preach the gospel to the poor. He has sent me to proclaim release to the captives, and recovery of sight to the blind, to set free those who are oppressed."

This is Jesus' ministry inaugurating announcement in the synagogue of his hometown, Nazareth. It is a quotation from Isaiah 61:1-2 which is a prophecy of the kingdom of God and should be interpreted as the Gospel of the Kingdom.

Luke 9:6 – Departing, they began going throughout the villages, preaching the gospel and healing everywhere.

Although Luke only has Gospel here, he has the Gospel of the Kingdom in mind because in 9:2 Jesus sends them out to proclaim the Gospel of the Kingdom.

Luke 20:1 – On one of the days while He was teaching the people in the temple and preaching the gospel, the chief priests and the scribes with the elders confronted Him,

Acts 8:25 – So, when they had solemnly testified and spoken the word of the Lord, they started back to Jerusalem, and were preaching the gospel to many villages of the Samaritans.

In light of 8:12 where Luke says Philip was preaching the Gospel of the Kingdom, this verse should be interpreted that way as well.

Acts 8:40 – But Philip found himself at Azotus, and as he passed through he kept preaching the gospel to all the cities until he came to Caesarea.

In light of 8:12 where Philip was preaching the Gospel of the Kingdom, this verse should be interpreted that way as well.

Acts 14:7 – And there they continued to preach the gospel.

Acts 14:15 – And saying, "Men, why are you doing these things? We are also men of the same nature as you, and preach the gospel to you that you should turn from these vain things to a living God, who made the heaven and the earth and the sea and all that is in them."

In light of the context and the content of Paul's message to turn from idols to the living God, this use of Gospel should be interpreted in light of the Gospel of God.

Acts 14:21 – After they had preached the gospel to that city and had made many disciples, they returned to Lystra and to Iconium and to Antioch,

Acts 15:7 – After there had been much debate, Peter stood up and said to them, "Brethren, you know that in the early days God made a choice among you, that by my mouth the Gentiles would hear the word of the gospel and believe."

Acts 16:10 – When he had seen the vision, immediately we sought to go into Macedonia, concluding that God had called us to preach the gospel to them.

Romans 1:15 – So, for my part, I am eager to preach the gospel to you also who are in Rome.

Romans 1:16 – For I am not ashamed of the gospel, for it is the power of God for salvation to everyone who believes, to the Jew first and also to the Greek.

Romans 2:16 – On the day when, according to my gospel, God will judge the secrets of men through Christ Jesus.

In Chapter 5 we discussed 1 Corinthians 15 and whether the Gospel is only about Jesus' death and resurrection. I concluded that the Gospel in 1 Corinthians 15 is also about the enthronement of Jesus. Here is indication that the Gospel message is also about the judgment to come.

Romans 10:15 – How will they preach unless they are sent? Just as it is written, "how beautiful are the feet of those who bring good news of good things!"

This is a quote from Isaiah 52:7 and the "good things" are the fact that the Lord reigns. It is a Gospel of the Kingdom verse.

Romans 10:16 – However, they did not all heed the good news; for Isaiah says, "Lord, who has believed our report?"

Romans 11:28 – From the standpoint of the gospel they are enemies for your sake, but from the standpoint of God's choice they are beloved for the sake of the fathers;

Romans 15:20 – And thus I aspired to preach the gospel, not where Christ was already named, so that I would not build on another man's foundation;

In the larger context Paul uses Gospel of God in 15:16, Gospel of Christ in 15:19 and just Gospel here in 15:20 showing the different dimensions of the one Gospel that he preached.

Romans 16:25 – Now to Him who is able to establish you according to my gospel and the preaching of Jesus Christ, according to the revelation of the mystery which has been kept secret for long ages past,

1 Corinthians 1:17 – For Christ did not send me to baptize, but to preach the gospel, not in cleverness of speech, so that the cross of Christ would not be made void.

1 Corinthians 4:15 – For if you were to have countless tutors in Christ, yet you would not have many fathers, for in Christ Jesus I became your father through the gospel.

1 Corinthians 9:14 – So also the Lord directed those who proclaim the gospel to get their living from the gospel.

1 Corinthians 9:16 – For if I preach the gospel, I have nothing to boast of, for I am under compulsion; for woe is me if I do not preach the gospel.

1 Corinthians 9:18 – What then is my reward? That, when I preach the gospel, I may offer the gospel without charge, so as not to make full use of my right in the gospel.

1 Corinthians 9:23 – I do all things for the sake of the gospel, so that I may become a fellow partaker of it.

1 Corinthians 15:1 – Now I make known to you, brethren, the gospel which I preached to you, which also you received, in which also you stand,

2 Corinthians 4:3 – And even if our gospel is veiled, it is veiled to those who are perishing,

The context for this verse is rich. In 4:4 Paul speaks of the Gospel of the glory of Christ which points to Jesus' resurrection and enthronement at the right hand of God, a Kingdom of God emphasis. In 4:4 he also speaks of Christ being the image of God which points to the Gospel of God. In 4:5 Paul says he proclaims Christ as Lord (Gospel of the Kingdom) and in 4:6 he goes back to the creation story pointing to the Gospel of God. He finishes by saying God's glory is found in the face of Christ.

2 Corinthians 8:18 – We have sent along with him the

brother whose fame in the things of the gospel has spread through all the churches;

2 Corinthians 10:16 – So as to preach the gospel even to the regions beyond you, and not to boast in what has been accomplished in the sphere of another.

2 Corinthians 11:4 – For if one comes and preaches another Jesus whom we have not preached, or you receive a different spirit which you have not received, or a different gospel which you have not accepted, you bear this beautifully.

Galatians 1:6 – I am amazed that you are so quickly deserting Him who called you by the grace of Christ, for a different gospel

Galatians 1:8 – But even if we, or an angel from heaven, should preach to you a gospel contrary to what we have preached to you, he is to be accursed!

Galatians 1:9 – As we have said before, so I say again now, if any man is preaching to you a gospel contrary to what you received, he is to be accursed!

Galatians 1:11 – For I would have you know, brethren, that the gospel which was preached by me is not according to man.

Galatians 2:2 – It was because of a revelation that I went up; and I submitted to them the gospel which I preach among the Gentiles, but I did so in private to those who were of reputation, for fear that I might be running, or had run, in vain.

Galatians 2:5 – But we did not yield in subjection to them for even an hour, so that the truth of the gospel would remain with you.

Galatians 2:7 – But on the contrary, seeing that I had been entrusted with the gospel to the uncircumcised, just as Peter had been to the circumcised

Galatians 2:14 – But when I saw that they were not straightforward about the truth of the gospel, I said to Cephas in the presence of all, "If you, being a Jew, live like the Gentiles and not like the Jews, how is it that you compel the Gentiles to live like Jews?

Galatians 3:8 – The Scripture, foreseeing that God would justify the Gentiles by faith, preached the gospel beforehand to Abraham, saying, "all the nations will be blessed in you."

Galatians 4:13 – But you know that it was because of a bodily illness that I preached the gospel to you the first time;

Ephesians 3:6 – To be specific, that the Gentiles are fellow heirs and fellow members of the body, and fellow partakers of the promise in Christ Jesus through the gospel,

This is another context-rich verse. Paul speaks of Christ Jesus in verse 6 and the riches of Christ in 8. In verses 9-10 Paul speaks of God's creation including the creation of the powers in heavenly places. In verse 11 he speaks of God's eternal purpose and in 13 he speaks of the glory that awaits God's people. Clearly, we have all three components of the Gospel in this section.

Ephesians 6:19 – And pray on my behalf, that utterance may be given to me in the opening of my mouth, to make known with boldness the mystery of the gospel,

Philippians 1:5 – In view of your participation in the gospel from the first day until now.

Philippians 1:7 – For it is only right for me to feel this way about you all, because I have you in my heart, since both in my imprisonment and in the defense and confirmation of the gospel, you all are partakers of grace with me.

Philippians 1:12 – Now I want you to know, brethren, that my circumstances have turned out for the greater progress of the gospel,

Philippians 1:16 – The latter do it out of love, knowing that I am appointed for the defense of the gospel;

Philippians 1:27 – Only conduct yourselves in a manner worthy of the gospel of Christ, so that whether I come and see you or remain absent, I will hear of you that you are standing firm in one spirit, with one mind striving together for the faith of the gospel;

Philippians 2:22 – But you know of his proven worth, that he served with me in the furtherance of the gospel like a child serving his father.

Philippians 4:3 – Indeed, true companion, I ask you also to help these women who have shared my struggle in the cause of the gospel, together with Clement also and the rest of my fellow workers, whose names are in the book of life.

Philippians 4:15 – You yourselves also know, Philippians, that at the first preaching of the gospel, after I left Macedonia, no church shared with me in the matter of giving and receiving but you alone;

Colossians 1:5 – Because of the hope laid up for you in heaven, of which you previously heard in the word of truth, the gospel

Colossians 1:23 – If indeed you continue in the faith firmly established and steadfast, and not moved away from the hope of the gospel that you have heard, which was proclaimed in all creation under heaven, and of which I, Paul, was made a minister.

1 Thessalonians 1:5 – For our gospel did not come to you in word only, but also in power and in the Holy Spirit and with full conviction; just as you know what kind of men we proved to be among you for your sake.

This verse and the following in 2:4 must be interpreted in light in the three Gospel of God references in 2:2, 8, 9.

1 Thessalonians 2:4 – But just as we have been approved by God to be entrusted with the gospel, so we speak, not as pleasing men, but God who examines our hearts.

1 Thessalonians 3:6 –But now that Timothy has come to us from you, and has brought us good news of your faith and love, and that you always think kindly of us, longing to see us just as we also long to see you,

This is a generic use of good news.

2 Thessalonians 2:14 – It was for this He called you through our gospel, that you may gain the glory of our Lord Jesus Christ.

Here is a good instance of the Gospel pointing not only to the saving work of God in calling people to acknowledge his Son but also pointing them to the future of glory that he now experiences at the right hand of God.

2 Timothy 1:8 – Therefore do not be ashamed of the testimony of our Lord or of me His prisoner, but join with me in suffering for the gospel according to the power of God,

2 Timothy 1:10 – But now has been revealed by the appearing of our Savior Christ Jesus, who abolished death and brought life and immortality to light through the gospel,

2 Timothy 2:8 – Remember Jesus Christ, risen from the dead, descendant of David, according to my gospel,

This verse is interesting in that Paul describes Jesus' Davidic lineage as part of the Gospel. This is a reference to Israel's hope that God would bring their King into the world and, therefore, another connection with the Kingdom aspect of the Gospel.

Philemon 1:13 – Whom I wished to keep with me, so that on your behalf he might minister to me in my imprisonment for the gospel;

Hebrews 4:2 – For indeed we have had good news preached to us, just as they also; but the word they heard did not profit them, because it was not united by faith in those who heard.

Hebrews 4:6 – Therefore, since it remains for some to enter it, and those who formerly had good news preached to them failed to enter because of disobedience,

1 Peter 1:12 – It was revealed to them that they were not serving themselves, but you, in these things which now have been announced to you through those who preached the gospel to you by the Holy Spirit sent from heaven--things into which angels long to look.

1 Peter 4:6 – For the gospel has for this purpose been preached even to those who are dead, that though they are judged in the flesh as men, they may live in the spirit according to the will of God.

Appendix B – *The Gospel of God*

T his appendix contains ten explicit New Testament references to the Gospel of God. The comments in these verses show the relationship of the Gospel of God to the other components of the Gospel.

Mark 1:14 – Now after John had been taken into custody, Jesus came into Galilee, preaching the gospel of God.

In the next verse Jesus says that the Kingdom of God is at hand. The message of the Kingdom, therefore is a subset of the Gospel of God, the good news about this God who made all things.

Romans 1:1 – Paul, a bond-servant of Christ Jesus, called as an apostle, set apart for the gospel of God,

We should compare Paul being *set apart* for the Gospel of God with this verse in Galatians 1:15-16 where Paul uses the same language of being set apart to preach the Son among the Gentiles.

Romans 15:16 – To be a minister of Christ Jesus to the Gentiles, ministering as a priest the gospel of God, so that my offering of the Gentiles may become acceptable, sanctified by the Holy Spirit.

Paul uses the imagery of the Old Testament priesthood to illustrate his work. In the Old Testament a priest would offer sacrifices of praise to God. Here, Paul sees himself as a priest but instead of bringing an animal to God he brings Gentiles into the presence of God. Israel's function in the Old Testament was to show a world lost in idolatry the nature and character of the true God of the world. This is the Gospel of God. Paul is a minister of Christ Jesus which emphasizes the Gospel of Christ and the fact that Gentiles are leaving their rebellion behind and being brought into the worship of the one true God shows the goal of the Gospel of the Kingdom – the obedience of the nations. All three components work together.

2 Corinthians 11:7 – Or did I commit a sin in humbling myself so that you might be exalted, because I preached the gospel of God to you without charge?

Here Paul summarizes his ministry among the Corinthians as preaching the Gospel of God. In 1 Corinthians 2:2 he summarized it by saying that while among them he knew only Jesus Christ and him crucified.

1 Thessalonians 2:2 – But after we had already suffered and been mistreated in Philippi, as you know, we had the boldness in our God to speak to you the gospel of God amid much opposition.

1 Thessalonians 2:8 – Having so fond an affection for you, we were well-pleased to impart to you not only the gospel of God but also our own lives, because you had become very dear to us.

1 Thessalonians 2:9 – For you recall, brethren, our labor and hardship, how working night and day so as not to be a burden to any of you, we proclaimed to you the gospel of God.

The preceding three verses are one of the clearest expressions of Paul characterizing his ministry as proclaiming the Gospel of God. It makes sense that he would emphasize this in light of the idols from which the Thessalonians turned. 1 Thessalonians contains two other references to the Gospel in 1:5 and 2:4 while 2 Thessalonians contains one other reference to it in 2:13.

1 Timothy 1:11 – According to the glorious gospel of the blessed God, with which I have been entrusted.

1 Peter 4:17 – For it is time for judgment to begin with the household of God; and if it begins with us first, what will be the outcome for those who do not obey the gospel of God?

Revelation 14:6-7 – And I saw another angel flying in midheaven, having an eternal gospel to preach to those who live on the earth, and to every nation and tribe and tongue and people; 7 and he said with a loud voice, "Fear God, and give Him glory, because the hour of His judgment has come; worship Him who made the heaven and the earth and sea and springs of waters."

I placed this verse here even though it does not use Gospel of God. It is clear that this is a call to leave idolatry and to worship the Creator of all things.

Appendix C – *The Gospel of the Kingdom*

At first glance, the paucity of verses that couple the word *Gospel* with the word *Kingdom* may indicate that the preaching of the Kingdom was not that important or widespread. But as we showed in Chapter 4, the proclamation of the Kingdom was the central element in Christ's preaching. We discovered that the word kingdom was used 110 places in the Gospels and of these 110, 101 of them are statements in the mouths of the main Gospel characters. Of these 101, 94 are from the mouth of Christ.

We also learned that the Kingdom had tremendous significance such as it being the basis of all repentance, the first object of every man's pursuit, and the treasure to be sought above all else. Many places in the Gospels simply say that Christ proclaimed the Kingdom without using the word Gospel with it. We must also remember that after his resurrection the Kingdom formed the basis of his 40 days of instruction for the disciples.

We also discovered that the apostles proclaimed the Kingdom of God. We noted Philip preaching it in Samaria (8:12), and Paul preaching it on his journeys (14:22; 19:8; 20:25). In Acts 28:31, Luke's last verse he recorded Paul's preaching theme – "preaching the kingdom of God and teaching concerning the Lord Jesus Christ with all openness, unhindered."

Matthew 4:23 – Jesus was going throughout all Galilee, teaching in their synagogues and proclaiming the gospel of the kingdom, and healing every kind of disease and every kind of sickness among the people.

The Gospel writers seem to point to a three-fold action in

regard to the kingdom. It was preached or heralded, it was taught, and then its power was brought to bear upon need in the world which was usually, in the ministry of Christ, an act of healing or releasing people from demonic strongholds.

Matthew 9:35 – Jesus was going through all the cities and villages, teaching in their synagogues and proclaiming the gospel of the kingdom, and healing every kind of disease and every kind of sickness.

Matthew 24:14 – "This gospel of the kingdom shall be preached in the whole world as a testimony to all the nations, and then the end will come."

The parallel passage in Mark 13:10 simply says that the Gospel will be preached in all the nations.

Luke 16:16 – "The Law and the Prophets were proclaimed until John; since that time the gospel of the kingdom of God has been preached, and everyone is forcing his way into it."

Acts 8:12 – But when they believed Philip preaching the good news about the kingdom of God and the name of Jesus Christ, they were being baptized, men and women alike.

See Chapter 4 to see how this twofold message of the kingdom and the name of Jesus worked together.

Appendix D – *The Gospel of Jesus Christ*

Similar to the few references to the Kingdom of God in Appendix C, one might be surprised at the few references in the New Testament that link the word "Gospel" with "Jesus Christ". But this is because the Gospel writers most often used the shortened version, "The Gospel" or used other vocabulary such as "preaching the unfathomable riches of Christ" in Ephesians 3:8 and "proclaiming Him" in Colossians 1:28.

Mark 1:1 – The beginning of the gospel of Jesus Christ, the Son of God.

We have seen in other verses how the Gospel is not just the death and resurrection of Christ but his enthronement (1 Corinthians 15:20-28, his return in judgment (Romans 2:15) and that it points to the future glory of God's people (2 Thessalonians 2:14). Here we see Mark pointing to the Gospel's beginning in the ministry of John the Baptist who also preached the good news (Luke 3:18).

Romans 1:9 – For God, whom I serve in my spirit in the preaching of the gospel of His Son, is my witness as to how unceasingly I make mention of you,

Romans 15:19 – In the power of signs and wonders, in the power of the Spirit; so that from Jerusalem and round about as far as Illyricum I have fully preached the gospel of Christ.

In "Appendix B – The Gospel of God" we noted how the gospel of Christ and the Gospel of God worked hand-in-hand with Paul's ministry. Christ was the means by which rebellious Gentiles came back into the Kingdom and escaped the destruction of their idols and returned to the true God.

1 Corinthians 9:12 – If others share the right over you, do we not more? Nevertheless, we did not use this right, but we endure all things so that we will cause no hindrance to the gospel of Christ.

2 Corinthians 2:12 – Now when I came to Troas for the gospel of Christ and when a door was opened for me in the Lord,

2 Corinthians 4:4 – In whose case the god of this world has blinded the minds of the unbelieving so that they might not see the light of the gospel of the glory of Christ, who is the image of God.

In "Appendix A – The Gospel" we saw how this verse is contextually rich. It points to the work of Christ, to God's kingdom, and goes back to the creation story. The God of creation who first said, "Let there be light" spoke light again through Christ who is his perfect image. The God of creation was now speaking light through the apostles to people blinded by the darkness of the evil one.

2 Corinthians 9:13 – Because of the proof given by this ministry, they will glorify God for your obedience to your confession of the gospel of Christ and for the liberality of your contribution to them and to all,

2 Corinthians 10:14 – For we are not overextending ourselves, as if we did not reach to you, for we were the first to come even as far as you in the gospel of Christ;

Galatians 1:7 – Which is really not another; only there are some who are disturbing you and want to distort the gospel of Christ.

Philippians 1:27 – Only conduct yourselves in a manner worthy of the gospel of Christ, so that whether I come and see you or remain absent, I will hear of you that you are standing firm in one spirit, with one mind striving together for the faith of the gospel;

1 Thessalonians 3:2 – And we sent Timothy, our brother and God's fellow worker in the gospel of Christ, to strengthen and encourage you as to your faith,

2 Thessalonians 1:8 – Dealing out retribution to those who do not know God and to those who do not obey the gospel of our Lord Jesus.

It is interesting that the Gospel of Christ is not just to be believed but also to be obeyed. This ties in with Paul's emphasis in Romans 1:5 and 16:26 about the obedience of faith among the Gentiles and with Peter's same emphasis in 1 Peter 1:2.

Appendix E – *Other Descriptions of the Gospel*

Here are the other descriptions of the Gospel in the New Testament with the unique point that each makes in the letters and sermons of the apostles.

Acts 13:32 – "And we preach to you the good news of the promise made to the fathers."

We examined this verse and its context extensively in "Chapter 6 – The Apostles, God's Storytellers" and saw how Paul's Gospel message to the Jews and God-fearers in Pisidian Antioch (and presumably in all synagogues) was based in the history-long story of God's promises to Abraham, Isaac, and Jacob. Paul did not merely preach an individual salvation and a hope of people going to heaven when they die. He preached that the promises of God to the nation were fulfilled in the death and resurrection of Jesus of Nazareth.

Acts 20:24 – "But I do not consider my life of any account as dear to myself, so that I may finish my course and the ministry which I received from the Lord Jesus, to testify solemnly of the gospel of the grace of God."

For all of our preaching on grace (which is a good thing), we should find it interesting that this phrase is found only once in the New Testament. Of course, we also find over one hundred other uses of grace but this is the only place where the word "grace" and "Gospel" are linked in a verse. This phrase then finds less support than the Gospel of God and the Gospel of the Kingdom. Nevertheless, we do preach the grace of God in Christ along with the Gospel of God and the Kingdom.

Ephesians 1:13 – In Him, you also, after listening to the message of truth, the gospel of your salvation – having also believed, you were sealed in Him with the Holy Spirit of promise.

We noted in Chapter 3 that the word, salvation, meant much more than forgiveness of sins and justification for an individual. The Hebrew concept of salvation was a full-orbed concept that included salvation of the whole person, salvation of relationships, and salvation for the world. It would be similar to the Hebrew concept of *Shalom* which had the idea of wholeness and well-being for the whole person, the nation, and the world, including creation.

Ephesians 6:15 – And having shod your feet with the preparation of the gospel of peace.

The Hebrew word *Shalom* is behind the Greek word *eirene* when Paul speaks of the Gospel of peace. *Shalom* carries the idea of holistic peace, i.e., external as well as internal peace, peace for the whole man and eventually the cosmos.

Appendix F – *Preaching Good News*

In the preceding appendices, many verses which use the word "Gospel" are translating the verb, *euangelizomai*. An example would be Appendix C where Acts 8:12 is listed and speaks of Philip *proclaiming the good news* of the Kingdom.

Sometimes, however, the verb *euangelizomai* is translated "preach" or "proclaim" only. This often occurs when the sentence has another description of the good news that was preached. For example, 1 Corinthians 15:1 says, "Now I make known to you, brothers, the Gospel, which I *preached* to you. The word, "preached," is from *euangelizomai*, but it would be redundant and awkward to translate, "the Gospel which I preached as good news to you."

In Acts 8:4 we are told that those who had been scattered from the persecution in Jerusalem went about preaching the word. The word "preaching" is from *euangelizomai* and a literal translation would be "preaching the good news, the word."

In this appendix I have highlighted those verses which use *euangelizomai* but which are translated as "preached" or "proclaim" *only*. I amplified the translation to include "good news" or "gospel" and italicized the phrase. I also underlined the word or phrase that gives content to the good news. My goal in this appendix is to provide yet more textual evidence for the multi-dimensional presentation of the Gospel.

Luke 4:43 – "But He said to them, 'I must *preach the Gospel*, the kingdom of God to the other cities also, for I was sent for this purpose.'"

Luke 8:1 – "Soon afterward, He began going around from one city and village to another, proclaiming and *preaching the Gospel*, the kingdom of God."

Acts 5:42 – "And every day in the temple and from house to house, they kept right on teaching and *preaching the Gospel*, the Christ, Jesus."

Acts 8:4 – "Therefore, those who had been scattered went about *preaching the Gospel*, the word."

Acts 8:35 – "Then Philip opened his mouth, and beginning from this Scripture he *preached the Gospel* to him, this Jesus."

Acts 10:36 – "The word which he sent to the sons of Israel, *preaching the Gospel*, peace through Jesus Christ. He is Lord of all."

Acts 11:20 – "But there were some of them, men of Cyprus and Cyrene, who came to Antioch and began speaking to the Greeks also, *preaching the Gospel*, the Lord Jesus."

Acts 15:35 – "But Paul and Barnabas stayed in Antioch, teaching and *preaching the Gospel*, the word of the Lord."

Acts 17:18 – "And also some of the Epicurean and Stoic philosophers were conversing with him. Some were saying, 'What would this idle babbler wish to say?' Others, 'He seems to be a proclaimer of strange deities,' – because he was *preaching the good news*, Jesus, and the resurrection."

1 Corinthians 15:1-2 – "Now I wish to make known to you, brethren, the Gospel which I *proclaimed good news* to you, which also you received, in which also you stand. By which also you are saved, if you hold fast the word which I *proclaimed as good news* to you, unless you believed in vain."

Galatians 1:16 – "To reveal his Son in me so that I might *proclaim good news*, him, among the Gentiles...."

Galatians 1:23 – "But only they kept hearing, "He who once persecuted us is now *proclaiming the good news*, <u>the faith</u>, which he once tried to destroy."

Ephesians 2:17 – "And He came and *preached good news*, <u>peace</u> to you who were far away and peace to those who were near."

Ephesians 3:8 – "To me, the very least of all saints, this grace was given, *to preach good news* to the Gentiles, <u>the unfathomable riches of Christ</u>."

1 Peter 1:25 – "But <u>the word of the Lord</u> endures forever. And this is the word which was *preached as good news* to you."

Revelation 10:7 – "But in the days of the voice of the seventh angel, when he is about to sound, then <u>the mystery of God</u> is finished as he *preached the Gospel* to his servants the prophets.

We see that *euangelizomai, preaching the good news*, had content that emphasized all aspects of the Gospel.

- Kingdom of God – Luke 4:43; 8:1
- Mystery of God – Revelation 10:7

- The Word – Acts 8:4
- The Word of the Lord – Acts 15:35; 1 Peter 1:25

- The Faith – Galatians 1:23

- Christ Jesus – Acts 5:42
- Jesus – Acts 8:35
- Lord Jesus – Acts 11:20
- Jesus and the resurrection – Acts 17:18
- Him – Galatians 1:16
- Unfathomable riches of Christ – Ephesians 3:8

- Peace through Jesus Christ – Acts 10:36; Ephesians 2:17

- [That] by which you are saved – 1 Corinthians 15:1-2

About Jonathan Williams

Jonathan pastored for over 35 years and is now the president of Word of God, Speak – a teaching ministry that advances life change, builds a biblical worldview, and connects people to God's story of love for the world.

He is the Bible teacher for the daily program, *The Heaven & Home Hour* and the creator of and storyteller for *Stories of the Master*, a weekly radio broadcast heard around the world. *Stories of the Master* retells the story of Jesus and the stories he told bringing in historical and cultural details which modern people often miss, but details which make the stories come alive.

Jonathan was married to his first wife, Dee for 27 years. She is now with the Lord. They had three children and now have five grandchildren. Jonathan lives in San Antonio, Texas with his wife Kathleen, his co-worker and best friend.

For more information contact WGS Ministries at:

WGS ◆ PO Box 90047 ◆ San Antonio, TX 78209.
Email: info@WGSministries.org
www.WGSministries.org
1.210.717.6617

Also by Jonathan Williams

Resurrection Vision – The resurrection of Jesus proves He is who He claimed to be and that His work on the cross is enough to gain our forgiveness and justification, but what else does it mean? Learn all ten meanings of the resurrection of Jesus and strengthen your life with His resurrection power that is available to change us and the whole world for His glory.

Dead Men Rising: The Death of Sin | The Rise of Grace – In this detailed study that many are calling the best commentary on Romans 6, Jonathan probes the meaning of Paul's teaching on the death of the old man and the believer's death to sin and resurrection to a new life. Correcting centuries of misinterpretation, this book will set people free by guiding them to the only place of liberation – the death and resurrection of Jesus in behalf of his people. This book also has a companion study guide to help believers think through all that Paul said and how it applies to believers today.

Romans 9 and the Story Paul Was Telling – Like a majestic peak, Romans 9 stands before the explorer of biblical truth. Its beauty beckons us, but its slopes present many dangers for the unfamiliar traveler. Long a proof text passage for the Calvinist/Arminian debate, could it be that Romans 9 was really about something else? What was Paul's aim in Romans 9? What was the story he was telling his generation?

The Women Jesus Loved – Taking ten stories from the Stories of the Master program where Jesus interacted with women, The Women Jesus Loved dramatically presents the liberating love of Jesus to women in his time. This book shows the difference between Christ and every other person in the treatment of women and is crucial for the time in which we live where people are becoming aware of the plight of women in the world who suffer simply because they are women and vulnerable. Each chapter in this book contains questions for personal reflection or small group study.

The Prodigal Son and His Prodigal Father – Most people have heard of the prodigal son, but who was the prodigal father? In this retelling of Jesus' timeless tale, Jonathan Williams reveals who the true prodigal in the story is, explains why forgiveness can be such a hard gift to give, and how you can experience forgiveness in all its dimensions. The rich cultural and historical insights from the first century make the story come alive for readers today.

The Prodigal Son and His Prodigal Father can also be ordered in Spanish and Mandarin.

Grace for Every Day – We know the grace of God is one of the most important concepts in the Bible. But what does it mean and how do we get it in our lives? In this 7-part study, ideal for personal reflection or small groups, Jonathan takes a fresh, biblical look at God's grace and explains in practical terms how it can be part of our daily experience to empower us to live for God's glory.

You can order all books by calling 1.210.717.6617 or by ordering online at www.WGSministries.org/Shop.

Stories of the Master

S*tories of the Master* is Jonathan Williams' weekly storytelling program. He incorporates historical and cultural details from the works of scholars such as Dr. Kenneth Bailey and Gary Burge. Dr. Bailey spent 40 years living and teaching New Testament in Egypt, Lebanon, Jerusalem, and Cyprus. He is the emeritus research professor of Middle Eastern New Testament studies for the Tantur Ecumenical Institute in Jerusalem and is the author of many enlightening works including *Jesus Through Middle Eastern Eyes*. Dr. Gary Burge is professor of New Testament at Wheaton College and the author of numerous books including *Jesus: The Middle Eastern Storyteller*.

Stories of the Master is heard worldwide on Trans World Radio and in Albania, Kosovo, and Nepal in their native languages. You can hear all the stories online at www.StoriesoftheMaster.com. The goal of this storytelling program is to introduce people to Jesus of Nazareth. The events in his life and the stories he told are among the most famous in the world. It is our belief and hope that as people hear of Jesus, his power over sickness, evil spirits, sin, and death, they will be attracted to him and want to learn more about his mission to establish the kingdom of God and his vision for the world.

You can bring Jonathan to your church to hear these stories live. People have always loved stories. It's time for the world to hear again, *The Stories of the Master*! Contact him at PO Box 90047 – San Antonio, TX 78209 or call 1.210.717.6617.